A Woman in Business

A Woman in Business

The Life of Beatrice Fox Auerbach

Virginia Hale

Library of Congress Control Number: 2008907597
ISBN: Hardcover   978-1-4363-6614-4
                Softcover   978-1-4363-6613-7

Cover portrait courtesy of The Jewish Historical Society of Greater Hartford

Photos on pages 29, 64, 156 and 163—courtesy of The Jewish Historical Society of Greater Hartford

Photos on page 83 and 268 courtesy of the Hartford History Center, Hartford Public Library

Photo on page 120 courtesy of The Connecticut Historical Society, Hartford, CT

Photos on pages 75 and 260 courtesy of The University of Hartford Library Archive

All other images drawn from the family collection.

Cover design by Elisa G. Hale

This book was printed in the United States of America.

To order additional copies of this book, contact:
Xlibris Corporation
1-888-795-4274
www.Xlibris.com
Orders@Xlibris.com
50286

Dedicated to Elisa, Susanna and Olivia
Three extraordinary women

CONTENTS

Preface

The recollection is vivid. I was eight years old wearing my best-starched cotton dress and my patent leather Mary Janes. With my mother, I boarded a bus in Windsor headed for Hartford and a visit to G. Fox Department Store.

I can still see the splendid display windows facing Main Street, smell the wonderful fragrance from the cosmetic counters, and savor the memory of a post shopping lunch in the Connecticut Room. A trip to G. Fox was always an event, and once in a while my mother would point out a small well-dressed woman, saying, "That's Mrs. Auerbach. She is the owner of this store."

During her life, Beatrice Auerbach eschewed interviews about herself. "Write about the store, not about me," she would say. As a consequence, the abundance of published material about Mrs.

Auerbach is focused on the store or on her civic and philanthropic activities. When I approached her grandchildren about writing a biography, they responded with enthusiasm and provided me with a treasure trove of written material—personal journals, diaries, and correspondence—that opened the door to the host of experiences that form the backbone of this book.

In her private life, Beatrice Auerbach suffered a number of hardships, among them the loss of her husband before she was forty years of age, the stillbirth of twin girls, and breast cancer resulting in a complete mastectomy. And she had to walk the tightrope between being a woman and being a public figure at the helm of what was at one time the largest privately owned department store in the nation. As a woman, and as a Jew, she faced hostility in some circles, and she worked tirelessly to overcome those prejudices. With a six-million-dollar gift, she endowed the Service Bureau for Women's Organizations whose purpose was to educate women about their opportunities to shape their own lives and influence the lives of others. Though the Service Bureau marked her as an important protofeminist, it was only one example of the social action to which she devoted herself.

Early in her tenure as chief executive of G. Fox & Company, Beatrice promoted some of her black employees to sales positions rather than keeping them in menial roles. Hers was the first U.S. department store to do so.

She was in the vanguard of efforts to improve the welfare of her employees. Among other things, she initiated a five-day workweek, established an on-site infirmary, provided medical benefits, and began a contributory retirement plan as well as an interest-free revolving loan fund for employees in need. During the Depression, no one lost his/her position; and it was Mrs. Auerbach who, with the counsel of University of Connecticut advisors, designed a plan whereby World War II veterans would be reintegrated into their former positions with the store.

Among her friends were Chase Going Woodhouse, congresswoman from Connecticut, and Mrs. Eleanor Roosevelt. With Mrs. Woodhouse she traveled to all parts of the globe. She shared a warm friendship with Mrs. Roosevelt, which is captured in a series of letters between the two.

She was witness to two world wars and espoused an ethos which has virtually disappeared in our time. Not only did she consider her employees to be like family (and vice versa), but she also believed her customers deserved the best goods and services possible. The level of respect and loyalty engendered by those attitudes is cause for nostalgia from the vantage point of the twenty-first century, and their loss is not to be taken lightly.

This book celebrates the singular life of Beatrice Fox Auerbach as well as the times in which she lived it.

Acknowledgements

A great many individuals shared their memories and stories of Beatrice Fox Auerbach. Among them were Elaine Lowengard, Joan Kohn, Henry Scherer, Janet Harmon, Phyllis Katz, Beatrice Kramer, Trudi Lovell, Margery Hartman Oakes, Jane Keller Herzig, Mary Barry, James Elsner, James Kinsella, Eunice Kelly, Ann Uccello, Hinda Fischer, Rabbi Stephen Fuchs, Stephen B. Goddard, Eugene Gaddis, John Trahan, Mike Peters, Judith Pinney, and Shirley Koplowitz.

I also owe a debt to the librarians at the Jewish Historical Society, the Connecticut Historical Society, the Hartford Public Library, the State Library of Connecticut, the University of Hartford and the Dodd Research Center at the University of Connecticut.

Thanks to Sandra Katz and Martha Keener for their careful, critical reading of the text.

Most importantly, I am grateful for the generosity of Rena and Brooksie Koopman, who shared private journals, letters, photographs, and recollections of their remarkable grannie.

FIRE!

It was 11:15 PM on January 29, 1917, as the after theater crowd spilled into the Hartford streets. Two clerks, coming from the Palace Theater, saw a wisp of smoke emanating from the small passageway between the Brown Thomson Building and G. Fox & Company. One of the men, Peter Rothschild, ran across Main Street for a closer look and was greeted by dark smoke billowing from a basement window. He and his companion, M. J. Dunn, a clerk at G. Fox, ran to the alarm box on the corner of Church and Main. Sprinting back across the street, Rothschild saw that the entire side of the building facing the alley was engulfed in flames shooting up from the rear of the building some twenty to fifty feet. Soon fire companies from

Hartford and surrounding towns were battling the blaze.

Across Main Street stood a diminutive young woman with her arms around her father. She was Beatrice Fox Auerbach, and he was Moses Fox, the owner of G. Fox & Company. Tears filled their eyes as they saw the big department store going to ruin. By 11:45 PM, the Talcott Street building was a mere shell, and the building facing Main Street was a roaring inferno. Beatrice, then thirty years old, married, and the mother of a daughter, finally led her father away when he seemed on the verge of collapse.

Many citizens took an active part in preventing the spread of the fire. Some were pressed into service on Main Street, but more of them were assisting in fighting the advance of the fire to buildings in the rear. "Several evening suits were drenched in water careening off buildings."[1] People from the outskirts of the city made their way downtown via taxi, private automobile, the few streetcars that were operating, or on foot. Police were on hand to manage the sizeable crowd.

Stories about the fire consumed the two Hartford papers—the *Hartford Courant* and the

Daily Times—for days after the event.[2] Accounts were prolific of the heroic behavior of firefighters: Several firemen fought the blaze from the roof of Brown Thomson's, a four-story edifice to the south of G. Fox, and the lives of many firemen who attacked the blaze at close range were constantly threatened by falling windows and timbers.

The *Times* described the actions of men, women, and children, alert to prevent the spreading of the fire to the tenements north of the store, "armed with axes, brooms and almost everything conceivable to beat out the small fires that repeatedly started as a result of sparks flying in every direction."[3] It was thought that snow on the tenement roofs helped to save them.

From the very beginning, the papers theorized that the blaze was set. The headline of the *Times* on January 30, 1917, read, "Suspicion that Firebug Started Blaze which Resulted in the Loss of $750,000." And the front-page story declared, "Following as it did fourteen incendiary fires within a period of only a little over two weeks and attempts to burn the department stores of Brown Thomson and Wise-Smith & Co., on Saturday night, January 13, the probability of a fire maniac's hands touching off the conflagration [that proved the second greatest in Hartford's history] at once came under serious consideration."[4] Deputy Fire Chief M. Dahill said that the blaze, which was fully involved when firemen arrived, started on the bottom floor, and that could best be explained by incendiary origin. So certain were the authorities that an arsonist was on the loose in Hartford that they posted a complement of supernumerary policemen to augment the group of watchmen already assigned to G. Fox and the surrounding area.

The day after the fire, the *Courant* described the inside of the G. Fox building as "a pile of rubbish with absolutely no hope of salvage."[5] Moreover, while Mr. Fox had a number of insurance policies, there was none to cover the damage from fire, smoke, and water.

For a brief time, Moses Fox contemplated terminating the business in Hartford. But two days after the conflagration, an announcement appeared in the *Hartford Courant* which said, "We shall resume business just as soon as we can secure a suitable temporary store, details of which will be given as early as possible. The site of the store just destroyed will be utilized for a new establishment, which will be erected with the most dispatch compatible with the best construction and plans that will provide for every modern device and convenience. We take this occasion to express our gratitude to the trading public."[6]

On the same day that the announcement appeared, it was reported that all employees would remain on the payroll even though their place of employment would not be ready for them to resume working for some time. On the morning of January 30, employees gathered on the eighth floor of the G. Fox storehouse on the north side of Talcott Street. James F. Morrissey, then store supervisor, told those assembled, "There is one word in the language which tells its own story, and tells of what is best in life, and that word is *loyalty*. You have helped the firm, and the firm has helped you and will help you now at the moment when help means everything." Morrissey told the employees to report daily at 39 Allyn Street where the chief timekeeper would record their time and would pay them each week. With a staff of more than one thousand, it is estimated that the resulting payroll was to be "up in the five figures." Such commitment to its workforce and to the Hartford community was a hallmark of the Fox style of doing business. That loyalty would prove itself remarkable in the weeks that followed.

The store was out of service for what seemed barely a heartbeat. Though Mr. Fox was urged by friends not to try to rebuild, he was a civic-minded man profoundly interested in the city of Hartford. To keep his business alive, he rented every available space in the city, including a vacant church. And on February 2, 1917, the Board of Aldermen of the City of Hartford voted to allow G. Fox to occupy two floors of the Old State House, where "light articles only would be sold."[7] A short time later, a two-story building was erected at 83-85 Church Street, where some departments were consolidated. The *Hartford Times* reported that the firm had had rebuilding plans in mind for the last ten years. As evidence, they pointed to purchases such as the Neal, Goff, and Ingles buildings on Church Street, Tucker's on Trumbull Street, and Goodwill Hall on Pratt Street.

Since the store's warehouse was not totally affected by the fire, Mr. Fox had some inventory on hand, but the stock was at a low ebb following the holidays; and no spring shipments had yet arrived, so he immediately ordered inventory with which he stocked various "departments" across the city: notions on Church Street, furniture on Allyn Street, and corsets in the church basement. One of the small storefronts on Pratt Street served as a temporary business office and was the site of an extraordinary experience that confirmed the special bond between the citizens and the store. The fire had destroyed records of sales made and accounts due, including bills for Christmas shopping, so the management had no way of requiring payment for purchases. One by one, people began to appear at the business office saying, "I think I owe you this sum," and they paid their bills, as Beatrice was later to say, "From their hearts as well as their pocketbooks." Management estimated that over 90 percent of the accounts were paid in this display of honesty and devotion to G. Fox. On the site of the fire, an eleven-story building rose like the phoenix; and less than a year later, G. Fox & Co. was open for the Christmas rush.

IN THE GENES

Beatrice Fox Auerbach came by her mercantile skills naturally. Her family on both sides were in the business of selling goods. Her maternal grandfather, Ferdinand Stern, came to America in 1852 from Burkatzfeldan, Germany, at the age of twenty-two. He did not know the language or the customs of the state of New York where he settled. He took a peddler's pack and traveled the region selling his wares. There is an old Connecticut proverb that says, "The best school in which to have a boy learn human nature is to permit him to be a peddler for a few years." Utopian philosopher Bronson Alcott took a peddler's job rather than attend college. Collis B. Huntington, Harwinton, Connecticut's fabled financier, who established, with Leland Stanford, such railroads as the Central

Pacific and the Baltimore and Ohio, began his career as a peddler. As Peter Hughes, writing in the *Connecticut Lyric* about the Yankee peddlers, remarks, "From Huntington's peddler's pack grew a vast railroad empire"[1] And the American retailing system planted its roots on the peddler's trail.

In 1857, Ferdinand Stern opened a dry goods and millinery store in Newburgh, New York. An article memorializing him said, "Mr. Stern was a born merchant. From the start, he handled a superior grade of merchandise, and his prices were always a trifle lower than those of his competitors. He was quick to take advantage of any opportunity the market afforded him. His success in building up the business, which now bears his name, is attributable largely to the close personal attention and the untiring energy he gave to it. Up until the day he was taken sick with the disease that caused his death, he was to be seen in the store, and little went on that he did not know of. Added to this, he was of sterling integrity in all financial transactions. He left a name in the business world that his family and friends are proud of."[2]

Beatrice's paternal grandfather, Gerson Fox (born Gershon Fuchs), was the founder of that Hartford store which bore his name. The day he set foot on the soil of Connecticut, he knew his future was here. He, too, led the peddler's life for a time. Then, "one day in the spring of 1846, a sign appeared on the gambrel-roofed Samuel Tudor house . . . GERSHON FOX—FANCY GOODS"; and an advertisement appeared in the *Hartford Courant*, "Dealer in French, German, English, and American fancy goods. Silk, fringes, cravats, collars, ribbons, edging, veils, etc. Call and see our fresh goods arriving weekly from New York . . . Particular attention given to calls from the ladies." There was a rustle of silk skirts over the threshold of the little shop where myriads of drawers held tempting bits of finery. "And when the sun sank behind Talcott Mountain, oil lamps twinkled through the small panes of leaded glass." Thus began G. Fox and Company.[3]

When Gerson Fox passed away in August of 1880, the *Hartford Times* celebrated him as a man of scrupulous honor whose business dealings earned him "an enviable reputation among metropolitan wholesale houses." His affection for his family was cited as well-known by all acquainted with him. He left three sons and a daughter, all of whom were actively engaged in the retail trade. A fifth child, Anna Fox, predeceased him. His son Leopold Fox, and his son-in-law, I. Plaut, established Fox and

Plaut in Newark, New Jersey. Isaac and Moses Fox worked with their father in Hartford at the Main Street emporium. At the time of his death, Gerson was working on the four-story Main Street store, which eventually became G. Fox & Company.

Little is recorded about Beatrice's grandmothers except to say they both produced a number of children. Fannie Kurtz, the wife of Ferdinand Stern, was the mother of twelve; and Hannah Bamberger, wife of Gerson Fox, had a family of five. Three sons went into the retail trade, and Emma Fox married a retailer from New Jersey. Moses Fox took over the family business in 1880 on the death of his father.

In 1880, at age thirty, Moses married Sophie Kurtz who was eleven years younger than himself. Sophie died in 1883, ten days after giving birth to a daughter, also named Sophie. The child lived only ten years, dying in March of 1893 of diphtheria. On June 30, 1886, Moses took his second wife, Theresa Stern, who was ten years younger than Moses.

Theresa was a full-figured, dark-eyed brunette. Moses was of medium height with light brown hair and a wide smile. They were married at her parents' home in Newburgh, New York. Rabbi Winthrop of Brooklyn performed the ceremony. After the marriage, the couple took up residence at 534 Prospect Avenue in Hartford.

Moses and Theresa at home

On July 17, 1887, Beatrice Fox was born. Her
birth certificate gives her name as Hannah Beatrice

Fox, but Beatrice hated her first name and adopted her middle name very early in life. Because she was so tiny, her father called her Bits. On July 4, 1896, a second daughter was born to Moses and Theresa and was named Fannie.

Beatrice and her half-sister, Sophie

Beatrice was devoted to her half-sister, Sophie, and Sophie was a favorite of Beatrice's mother, Theresa. Beatrice was devastated when Sophie passed away, and she even believed that her parents would have preferred it if Sophie had lived and she died.[4]

A world traveler, Moses took his two daughters along on many of his journeys abroad, exposing them to the culture and habits of several regions of the globe. These journeys helped to familiarize Beatrice with the art, architecture, and music of Europe. In fact, these periodic trips were really a substitute for the higher education Beatrice was not to have. As daughter of a prominent family, she attended local public and private schools, including the North School and the Belden Street School in Hartford and the Benjamin Deane School, a Jewish boarding and day school in New York City. She never received a high school diploma, and she used to joke that she hadn't graduated "even from Sunday school."

Very early in her life, Beatrice's parents established for her the habit of keeping a diary of special events and travels. Fortunately, some of the early trip diaries have been preserved by her family,

**Beatrice (left rear) at North School
learning to knit**

and they open a small window into her childhood
and adolescence. The earliest of the travel diaries,
written when she was eleven years old, describes
a trip to Europe with her father and mother, her
sister Fannie, and a Ms. Wilson who was taken along
as a companion for the children.

She began her account on June 13, 1899, with the
experience of taking the trolley to the Hartford Train
Station where they boarded a train to New York City.

Once in the city, they took another trolley, this time to the Waldorf-Astoria. Beatrice wrote, "We were all very dirty" on arrival, and after a satisfying dinner, the family retired to bed with "clean linens."

The next morning, the family went to the wharf by carriage to board the ship to Europe. They were met by many relatives and friends who had come to see them off. Beatrice and Fan spent the afternoon in their steamer chairs. In the morning, she was awakened by the breakfast bugle and came on deck just in time to see her vessel pass a cattle steamer.

At age eleven, Beatrice showed her sociability, making friends with a number of her shipmates. She played quoits and shuffleboard with another young girl, and she was defeated at checkers by one of the boys aboard. In her diary, she recorded that she spent some time playing the piano, a skill which she rarely mentioned again. On the third day of the voyage, she befriended a girl named Hazel, and the two walked the deck and conversed. "As it is Sunday, we aren't allowed to play games, so we sat on deck and read a book together."

The ship arrived in London on July 4, Fan's birthday. After settling in their rooms at the

DeKapers Royal Hotel, the family took a walk to St. Paul's Cathedral which, according to Beatrice, was "old and like all the other buildings here very dirty looking." In the evening, her parents went to the theater, and she took a "peachy bath."

She learned very early that adjustments must be made when one travels to another country, even when they speak the native language. In an encounter with a waiter, she asked to be directed to the hotel elevator; only after some discussion was she able to communicate to him that she wanted to find the lift.

Beatrice especially admired London's many gardens and found Hyde Park and Kensington Park "very pretty indeed." But she was not so impressed with London's fabled department stores remarking that "I do not think (they) come up to our stores in Hartford."

July seventeenth was her own birthday, and the family arranged a boat trip to Greenwich where they learned about the establishing of latitude and longitude and where Beatrice was so fascinated that she almost missed the return boat. The next day, they visited several hotels including the Metropole and the Victoria. At each of them, Beatrice took some monogrammed paper and stuck it under her blouse, out of sight. The value of the souvenir seems to have outweighed the risk of discovery.

The family took a tallyho tour (probably by stagecoach) of towns just outside of London. A luncheon was provided as part of the tour, but Beatrice was less than impressed. "It was highway robbery seeing it cost $4.00 for just five of us including Fan. I will tell you what we had: cold roast beef (nearly all of it was fat), nasty lettuce salads (just like grass), potatoes (all full of cooks' hairs), some pears (about ten years old), and some nasty ginger ale. Well, I tell you it was nearly as bad as *Ten Nights in a Bar Room*."

Before leaving London, the family visited the Tower where Beatrice was shown where the queens died, an experience which impressed her with the precarious nature of power. But she was bowled over by the crown jewels and promised herself to return someday and spend more time enjoying them.

On July 10, Ms. Wilson and the children went to Little Hampton where they were to stay at the Beach Hotel while their parents went to Norway and Sweden. The girls got bathing suits there, which were made without shirts, so her mother and Ms. W made shirts for them, and they went paddling. Beatrice wrote, "I caught quite a few crabs and was bit by quite a few." The next day, they purchased rubber bathing shoes because the beach was very stony.

During the absence of Mr. and Mrs. Fox, a certain Mr. H started to follow them around, apparently attracted to Ms. Wilson. Beatrice heartily disapproved. In fact, she disapproved of several people she encountered at Little Hampton. As a case in point, on August 9, after it had been raining for a few days, Ms. Wilson decided to take the girls for an early walk before the rain would begin again, which had been forecast. While they were out, the precipitation started in earnest, so they sought shelter in a nearby cottage. "There the lady had peaches, apples, and grapes right in front of us, and she did not give us any. We came home rather wet," Beatrice complained.

Beatrice often commented on food in her diaries, and she was generous with her praise when it met with her approval. "I found the food there of the best it has been my good fortune to eat," but she was scathing in her criticism, as in the description of the tour luncheon.

After her parents returned, the family traveled on to Germany where she made careful note of décor and statuary in various palaces they visited. With a child's enthusiasm, she exclaimed over the stables at the Reichstag, which housed more than three hundred horses of different breeds. Gerson's store in Potsdam won her approval especially for the range and quality of the apparel for sale.

An early formal portrait of Beatrice

In 1908, the Fox family took a car trip through New England with the Plaut family. There were eight travelers: Moses and Theresa Fox, Moses's sister Emma Fox Plaut and her husband, and the four teenage girls Hortense and Blanche Plaut, Beatrice and Fannie Fox. A diary was written by Hortense Plaut.

The adventurers embarked from New York City in a rented sixty-horsepower Thomas Flyer. They were scarcely out of the city when Beatrice moved her head and accidentally struck the lamp, breaking her glasses in the process. They stopped in Hartford to have them repaired at G. Fox & Company's optical department.[5]

In 1908, the countryside in Connecticut was largely unsettled, and Hortense remarked on how quiet and how wild it was. "In Norfolk," she wrote, "you can hear the grass grow." The first of their stops was at the Red Lion Inn in Stockbridge, Massachusetts, to see the furnishings and old china. Afterward they headed for Pittsfield where they spent the first night.

Going through North Adams, "nothing more than a hole," they came to Williamstown where the college buildings impressed the entire group. That evening, they stayed over at Manchester, Vermont, where they had hoped to lodge at the Equinox; but because it was not yet open for the season, they stayed at the Orvis Cottage, which Beatrice found delightful because it was "a boarding house which gives the effect of a private home just offering you their hospitality." She was charmed by the authenticity of the antique furnishings and the expansive library. Moreover, there was no electricity, so lamps and candles offered the only light.

Beatrice and her sister Fannie

The three older girls read Schiller in German at night. On one occasion, they staged a kimono party "flattering ourselves," Hortense remarked, "that it was very picturesque."

Extended automobile travel was still something of a rarity in 1908. The group averaged between 90 and 110 miles a day, and they were on the road most days for nine or ten hours. Arriving in Burlington, Vermont, after a 110-mile trip mostly in the rain—at one point the girls had to exit the vehicle and walk up a hill to avoid sinking in the mud—they learned theirs was the very first car to visit that year.

The party moved on to White River Junction where they went to a hotel whose lobby was full of "men in all kinds of lolling postures, and there was a harp and a squeaky violin going full blast. It reminded me," Hortense wrote, "of a scene from Dickens' *Martin Chuzzlewit*."

In Laconia, New Hampshire, they bedded down in a room with no screens; and Beatrice, whom her cousin called Beats, awakened with swollen eyelids due to mosquito bites and for the next two days carried the Pond's Extract bottle in her coat pocket. To make matters worse, her mother warned her to abstain from eating strawberry shortcake; but she indulged anyway, and the result was "a first-rate case of hives."

All in the company applauded Boston as a lovely city with splendid suburbs with which, Beatrice said, "even a New Yorker can't find fault."

Beatrice and her cousin Hortense Plaut at the St. Bernard Pass

Their last stop before heading home was in Plymouth where the car's mainspring broke, and they were forced to spend an additional day. Hortense observed that it was a pleasant town where the sense of history abounds.

With her travel experience, Beatrice had early on developed an adventuresome character. Brooksie Koopman, her granddaughter, recalled her grannie's stories about participating in horse and carriage races down Main Street in Hartford as a young girl.

For much of her youth, Beatrice continued the practice of keeping a diary. In October of 1907, Beatrice entered the Benjamin Deane School, located at 144 Riverside Drive in New York. In her diary, she described herself as immediately homesick. Her aunt and her mother brought her to the school and helped get her settled. She hated to let them go, and the goodbyes were tearful.

Beatrice was assigned to a room shared with three other students, and initially she wasn't happy with the arrangement. Still she said, "The single rooms are too small," so she went about settling in. She described the place as "extremely dirty" and wondered if she could ever live there. Her

roommates were Juliet G. from Alabama, Blanche
from New Haven, and Adele D. from Rochester.
She described Juliet as "sweet and Southern,"
Blanche as "wordy," and Adele as "very bright."
As they gradually became better acquainted,
Beatrice seemed more at ease, though she quickly
objected to some of the rules; and when the
order was lights-out at 8:00 PM, the roommates
continued to chat until each of them dropped
off to sleep.

Every morning, Beatrice and her fellow
students had to "file downstairs two by two at the
ringing of the breakfast bell." Order and decorum
appeared to be of primary concern at Benjamin
Deane. Beatrice expressed uncertainty that she
was up to the level of some of her classes, and she
thought about changing her program. Whether
she did or not remains a secret since she made
no further reference to her studies in the diary.
She did say that one of her steady occupations
was playing bridge.

Apparently, even then, the city held dangers
for young women. The school rule was that no
girl could go out except "in larger groups so no
one will take you." Beatrice soon established the

habit of making outdoor forays. On one trip, she shopped at Macy's where her purchases included Hudnett's violet water, ribbon, toothpicks, and hairpins. From time to time, her relatives would visit and take her off for a meal or a ride. On one occasion, she described their trip to the suburbs as "leaving us all with the peck of dust we are all doomed to consume."

A letter from her mother, Theresa, dated May 7, 1907, suggested that Beatrice had quickly adjusted to New York. Theresa was firm about limiting Beatrice's social life in the city. "You cannot go out to the theater with Mrs. Hecht. I am surprised you ask. You know what I told you . . . it is high time you got home so I can have you under my thumb. Also accept no invitation to go out of the city with anyone. I don't want you to go out walking with any strange boys, not even those from here. Mind you do *exactly* as I want. I will hear things if you don't."

Theresa threatened Beatrice with losing the opportunity to be away from Hartford for the coming year and ended her letter, "Mind what I say and don't run after a pair of pants."

Clearly, Beatrice had her share of suitors. One, in particular, was Federico di Palma, an Italian politician from the town of Grottaglia in the province of Taranto in Southern Italy. Exactly when they met is not certain, but about eighty postcards document a two-year correspondence. Many cards were addressed to her in Europe and in Egypt, which she visited in the fall and winter of 1904-1905. While a few cards were written in English, the vast majority were in French, which they must have used as a common language. Di Palma apparently traveled all over Europe for business, which probably involved marine commerce, judging from one postcard. He was certainly enamored of her, but he was nearly twenty years her senior, and there is no evidence that they ever met again. In the fall of 1906, he wrote that perhaps they should break off the correspondence; and although there are a few cards dated later, they appear to be simple holiday greetings.

Beatrice remained at Benjamin Deane from 1907 to 1909, but her attendance was interrupted by trips abroad; and in 1909, the school yearbook indicated only that she "continued her art studies with Ms. Delmar."[6]

The Fox family in Switzerland

GEORGE AND BEATRICE

In 1907, onboard the USS *Olympia* sailing to Norway with her family, Beatrice met George Auerbach. Just two years her senior, George stood a head taller than Beatrice and was a natty dresser. He was of medium build, had a receding hairline, and wore glasses. George was the son of a retailer whose department store was the largest in Salt Lake City, Utah. He was the third of eight children. His grandparents, all Silesian immigrants, were among the first Jews to settle in Utah. The Auerbachs came to Salt Lake City as merchants, and they prospered. George, with two of his brothers, managed the family business.

Beatrice aboard the SS. Olympia

A letter sent to Hartford from Norway in August 1907 reported that the Fox and Auerbach families planned to leave Norway together, traveling by wagon to Stockholm. There were nine members of the Auerbach family and four of the Foxes. Certainly, the trip offered an opportunity for George and Beatrice to become better acquainted with one another and with their families; and Fannie, then eleven, got to know Frederick Auerbach whom she would marry in 1925. After marrying, Fan, like her sister before her, made her home in Salt Lake City, living there until Frederick's passing in 1938. Both George and Frederick died young, and although Beatrice never remarried, in September 1940, Fan married Leslie Samuels in Salt Lake City. They moved East, and Fan lived the rest of her life in New York City.[1]

George confessed to having been smitten with Beatrice at once, and in a letter written in 1910, he revealed that he had told his mother immediately that he intended to marry Beatrice. In his letter, he described the two of them sitting in their deck chairs under heavy coverings and holding hands.

From the time of their engagement, in August of 1910, until their marriage in April 1911, George and Beatrice corresponded daily. More than one hundred fifty letters written by George revealed a lot about their lives then and their plans for the future. In general, the majority of the letters fall into a pattern. In every one, he sent his love and affection to her, describing in detail how much he loved her and dreamed of their being together. Sometimes he seemed on the edge of desperation because they were not together, but he always reassured her that they would never be apart once they were wed.

A second recurring theme in the letters expressed his concern about taking her away from her parents and from the East to live in Salt Lake City. In these letters, he described life in the West, the promise he saw there, the community and its people, and, more specifically, where and how they would live.

A third constant theme in the letters was a description of his own day-to-day life.

In a letter dated September 27, 1910, George recounted a trip to the countryside to look at some land. George and four others departed before sunrise. The day was cold, so he began his account by describing his clothing. "I put on woolen underwear, heavy shoes, a flannel shirt, and on top of my vest and coat I wore an overcoat. Frank Kelly was the driver, and I told Claude Freed where to get all of the provisions which were ready for us, and we drove off to get Mr. Byron and Mr. Wallace, then down Main Street we came sailing . . . . We stopped for breakfast consisting of cantalope, three eggs and bacon, juice, and cream and coffee. Then we started. It was decided that Claude Freed's automobile would be better to make a trip in than mine, as he had better facilities for carrying provisions, gas, and oil than I had. He has a trunk on the rear of the car, and we loaded that with the provisions and some beer. On the running board, we had ten gallons of gasoline in tin cans. On the other side, we had the mechanics. We headed fairly rapidly toward the South over fairly good roads, and the cold air stung sharply but made us feel happy and full of life. We were soon traveling over a road that had never been made by an auto before in the history of that road. It really wasn't a road, we just picked our way across country after the first fifty miles. We drove amongst the sagebrush on the hills and the villages. You know, there is but little of that land that is farmed, so there was nothing to retard us except the occasional gullies or small gulches made by torrents and at times exceedingly hard to cross. When the sun came up, things felt much better. It was ten thirty when we reached our destination and looked over the land. Some of the land is very good, and most of the good land has already been spoken for. I haven't really decided what to do. The other land that is open is still good and worth more than it will cost me, but you understand each citizen has the privilege but once of taking up land as a homestead and I'd forfeit my privilege for the future if I exercised it now. I can see you pucker your eyes and say to yourself, 'Well then, I can take some up for mine.' But you cannot dearest as a man and wife are only allowed one homestead right, though single women have the same rights as men. I can't take some in your name before we get hitched as you must swear that you have been on the land. But enough of all that. We drove over the land, which covers an area of several square miles, and looked at the lands along the foot of the mountains as they are the best. There is water on the lands, and the only way to obtain it is by sinking a well. If one gets close to the base of the mountains, they contain a great deal of moisture coming from the melting of the snows that keeps moving toward the base of the mountains so that it is possible to conduct dry farming there where you won't succeed in other places.

"We had a puncture, so we decided to have lunch at the same time. Our water we carried in what are called South African water bags, and it was nice and cool. These bags, in case you haven't heard about them, are the invention of a clever mind and consist of a closely woven canvas. There is a very little evaporation of water through the very fine weaving of the canvas; it practically produces a vacuum in the bag, which results in the water cooling. The remarkable thing about them is the warmer the day, the cooler the water.

"We had a very hard trip of it coming back as we missed our road and simply had to drive for the mountains through sagebrush that stood from two to three feet in height. It took us about three hours to go ten miles, so you can imagine the fun. We got another puncture, and while Frank fixed the puncture, we put up targets and shot at them with a rifle and a revolver. It was eight thirty when we came in, covered with dust and tired out completely."

In a letter of December 31, 1910, George expressed his enthusiasm for Salt Lake City and its promise. "Beatrice, you are so full of fun and life and so loveable and such a dandy girl. Why partner you know we'll show them all a thing or two—just give us time. I may be a get rich quick Wallingford and may have gotten cold feet just like Wallingford[2] and ready to give us the slip, but now never. Things are too good and our carpet covered tracks are an assured success. Let me rave—it does me good to get it out of my system, but aside you my own sweetheart, know that Salt Lake is so situated as to be the central point between the East and the West, and some day we shall see the most wonderful change in this city. It will be a second Chicago as far as a railroad center is concerned.

"Why just stop and figure how many railroads leave or enter this city today and how many distinct lines leave here. There is a road to Los Angeles, two roads to San Francisco, one to Spokane, Portland and Seattle, and to Butte and to Logan and southern Idaho; one to Denver, one to Chicago, one to the Park City mining district, one to the Bingham Mining District, one to the Eureka Mining District and to Richfield, one to Manti. These are all separate tracks that meet in Salt Lake. Then the street railway company has suburban cars to Murry and Sandy and the Bamberger line runs to Ogden. Say, if I was writing a prospectus and you

were to read it, never having been out here, don't
you think you'd fall for it and wonder and think
of it? You'd begin to feel that the railroad people
regard our beautiful city as the center of the USA
and that with time all business from the East to the
West and visa versa would have to bear our stamp
of approval. Then let me call to your attention that
the Colorado Midland is now building into Salt
Lake—that the Moffat line is coming from Denver
and in a short time the Northwestern will be ready
to start work. Well then, come and join us in our
beautiful community of mutual good interests."

Of course, the railroads brought occasional
problems to the region. In one letter, George
urged Beatrice not to worry about the many
train robberies that had been written about in
the newspapers. He assured her he was okay
but wondered why the number of such events
increased during the winter.

George was one of eight children. His mother,
Eveline Brooks Auerbach, wrote a memoir entitled
Frontier Reminiscences[3] about the experiences
of her family as they made their way across the
country to Salt Lake City in 1857. Indeed, they were
pioneers in every sense of the word, traveling in

covered wagons as members of a train of fifteen wagons. More important, they were immigrant pioneers, having come from Germany to America, and Jews moving into a Mormon community. The *Utah History Encyclopedia* names Frederick and Samuel Auerbach, George's father and uncle, among the key figures in the business community, owning both a bank and a mercantile. Jewish men were active in public life soon after their arrival in Utah. The formation of the Salt Lake City Chamber of Commerce in 1887 recorded the names of J. E. Bamberger, M. H. Lipman, and Fred H. Auerbach as members. In 1916, Simon Bamberger would be elected governor of Utah, the first non-Mormon to hold that office.[4]

George's father established a dry goods store in Salt Lake, and when he came of age, George worked full-time in the store. No doubt, their similar backgrounds contributed to the strength of the bond between Beatrice and himself.

But for all the similarities, there were significant differences between Beatrice and George. One issue on which George frequently commented is the contrast between the financial resources of their respective families.

Anticipating her first visit to Salt Lake before their wedding, he urged her to ask all the questions she could think of. He wanted her to be satisfied with conditions before they married and moved to Utah. "So you won't expect more than you're getting when you marry me. You're giving up a fortune, you're giving up your family, and all for one boy out here in the West. You must understand that while my folks own a good deal of property, mining stocks, and the dry goods business, it must all be divided by eight, so I won't have a big fortune from them."

Elsewhere George worried about her possible extravagance in making purchases for her trousseau. He recognized she was not yet his wife, so it fell to her father to judge appropriate expenditures. But he worried that "the more show you put on now, and the less you put on afterward will be bound to cause gossip, and people will feel that you were a fool that married out of your class, and (your) Dad and Mother might feel the same way." He assured her (and himself) that "we'll prove to them that they were all wrong." On another occasion, he warned against too many fancy and delicate clothes, not particularly suited for life in

Utah. Here he was even more specific, suggesting she "buy things that are practical, that will last, that we can afford, and that you are going to buy later on. Don't you think that if you start off with beautiful lingerie that you will miss it later on?"

George was firm on certain principles. In January of 1911, he wrote, "You must not take the least assistance from your family even if we have to be stingy." He further insisted that anything her family gave her should go into a trust fund "for our kiddies."

George hastened to tell her how much he believed that he had the right stuff to make his mark in the world. And he reminded her of the success of his past and current ventures. "I hit this town when everyone was afraid of their own shadow. I felt fresh and young. I took chances, and everything I touched made money for me—to a certain extent I probably lost my head." Some investments clearly went wrong, and he told her it would probably be five years before he really felt secure and established, and he hoped that he would be able to pay off a big part of his father's indebtedness, "most of which has been incurred on my advice." Nevertheless, he continued to make investments that he believed would pay off handsomely, particularly in real estate.

In a letter dated February 8, 1911, George detailed a land purchase in Nevada, reassuring Beatrice that he had been careful and shrewd. "I'll be the largest owner of lands in this valley, and some of the lands are very fine." On a less venturesome plane he wrote to her about his work in the store where he and his brother Herbert were the key players. He told her that he must write briefly in December 1910 because he had to work on the sales floor during the Christmas rush. On Christmas Eve, they would keep the store open until ten thirty. "You know the last customers are the best ones. They haven't time to shop, and they usually buy the best things."

On September 20, 1910, George wrote about a new opportunity. "I was called away by one of our tenants who wanted to see me. It was the saloonkeeper on State Street opposite the Huntsford, and he told me of some land being opened to settlers. The land is in this state right on the railroad and costs but $24.00 for 360 acres. In addition to this twenty-four, it is necessary to give one hundred dollars to one of the men who has the surveys etc. and who knows the property to a T and who offers to let me in on the deal. You know, when the government opens ground to home seekers this way, it is necessary that a man can swear that he has been on the ground, and it is also necessary to cultivate forty acres inside of one year. There is very little of such land to be had these days. I naturally told the saloon man that I was in on the deal, and I asked him to let Mr. Wallace in, which he agreed to do. The one big and important thing to know is just when this land will be thrown open. Now by forming a pool and paying one hundred each, we can employ a man whose duty it is to await the opening of these lands; and as soon as they are open for entry, he notifies us from the nearest telephone. Then we beat it to the office of the land register, leave, and locate. Those who are too late get their $100.00 refunded. The minute we get this land—if we get it—it is worth about a thousand dollars or more depending on its location. Whether we can get artesian wells on the ground etc. by which I mean proximity to a town, to a county road, to the railroad, and dependent on the soil of the land. Mr. Wallace and I go down there on Tuesday."

George was not above offering financial advice to Beatrice's father. On one occasion, Moses asked, through Beatrice, about the price of linens in Salt Lake, and George responded in some detail. At another time, George told Beatrice to speak to her father who owned stock in Wells Fargo and Adams Express. He had heard that the Congress was considering a bill called Parcel Post, which, if passed, would reduce the express companies' role in delivering packages. In October of 1910, in a letter to Beatrice, he sent stock tips on mining to Moses.

Much of George's enthusiasm derived from his belief in Utah itself. In October of 1910, he described for her "Conference Week when all of the good saints from the surrounding country swarm to the city to hear the president of the Mormon Church tell them what the will of their Lord is." Naturally business was fine as a result. He celebrated Utah for all of its resources and opportunities and called it "one of the paradises on earth." Of course, the development of the railroads put Salt Lake City in the center of transit and the commerce attendant to it. George confessed his boyhood dream to own a railroad, but he recognized it was beyond him at the moment. Still he did all he could to capitalize on the opportunities the railroads offered. He was part of a committee petitioning the railroads to allow ten-day stopovers on all trips passing through Salt Lake. And he was eager to entertain the many people who would travel through Salt Lake on their way to the World's Fair in San Francisco. The Panama Canal, too, he saw in its relationship to Salt Lake City, telling Beatrice that he believed "Utah will profit enormously by the worldwide trade that will come about."

A number of letters from George discussed directly arrangements for Beatrice's move from Hartford. He instructed her to purchase a trunk and outlined the luggage he thought they would need to travel to Utah after the wedding. From time to time, he offered sketches of the layout of certain apartments they might consider. He told her that one of the hotels might be best at the start, but "there are issues." At the Blansford, they could get a furnished apartment but must eat meals there. "If you furnish your own apartment, you have to do your own housekeeping." He said the best apartments were at the Twinball, where they would have five rooms and bath for $75.00 per month. Beatrice had apparently made some specific requests. In response to her desire for a pantry, he wrote, "Out here it isn't customary to have a pantry as all of the glasses and china for daily use are kept in the kitchen." He got this information from his family's cook.

From a number of postcards addressed to Beatrice in Salt Lake City, it is certain that the couple ultimately settled at the Blansford.

Certainly George enjoyed a full social life as a bachelor. He and four or five of his cronies gathered often to dine out and to go to the theater. The three theaters in the town offered road companies' performances. At various times, he described for her performances at the Orpheum, the Garrick, and the Colonial. The last of these was established by George himself. The site was property owned by his parents where George was born. For a time, the Northwestern Theatrical Association worried that there would not be enough theatergoers to support the first-rate playhouses, but they decided to lease the Colonial and bring to Salt Lake "first-rate yet popularly priced operas and dramas."[5] Among the plays George mentioned he had seen were *The Prisoner of Zenda*, *Broken Idol*, and *The*

Midnight Sun. He had seen Madame Bernhardt play Jeanne d'Arc and Annette Kellerman perform her diving exhibition. His enthusiasm for the theater emboldened him to make a suggestion for Moses Fox. "You know, dear, if we can get Mother and Dad to put up a moving picture house in Hartford that they can get good rent, and it won't cost them $10,000 to build one." No doubt he was speaking from experience, since his brother Herbert designed and built, kitty-corner from the store, the Centre Theatre, at the time the largest and one of the best-equipped motion picture houses in Salt Lake City.

Beatrice could certainly look forward to enjoying the theater in Salt Lake. But other entertainments about which George wrote are strictly male pursuits: duck hunting, boxing lessons, and trips to the Turkish bath among them.

In response to one letter, detailing his activities on New Year's Eve 1910, Beatrice apparently expressed her displeasure because there had been women in the group. He reassured her that the women were considerably older—thirty-five to forty-five—so she needn't worry. He insisted he was behaving, but he must sometimes accept social engagements. George too expressed a bit of jealousy about the boys who squired Beatrice in his absence. "I know the boys are brighter than I am in lots of ways, and I'm glad they are for we can't all be bright in the same thing, and I never claimed to be bright. I claimed and do claim to have nerve, to have confidence in our country and its growth, and to have the ability to talk up things that I sincerely believe in." Still he expressed his wish to give a party when he came East to thank Sol Elsner and the Hartman boys for escorting Beatrice around since he couldn't.

The wider community too offered George some opportunities to socialize. He sent her his invitation to a dance at the home of the Eccles, a prominent Salt Lake family, "so you can see that even the Jews get invited once in a while to a Mormon dance." He followed this with a comment that Beatrice would probably enjoy the society of the gentiles because the Jewish women seemed to lead uninteresting lives.

Responding to Beatrice's wishes, George told her that he was making some changes in his personal habits, "cutting down on meats and coffee, and reducing to two or three cigars a day." Elsewhere he advised her not to worry about him because he was "taking a tonic and using a hair restorer and getting plenty of sleep." He in turn urged her to try to be just like her mother, "for she is about my ideal of a perfect woman."

In what seems an unusual view for the times, George indicated frequently that he envisioned their marriage as a partnership. He showed this by asking her advice; for instance, in whether or not he should keep both of the life insurance policies he held or surrender one and acquire coverage for her. He promised to teach her to drive since both of them love to travel, and they "should do a lot of it." In a letter of October 28, 1910, George wrote that Atty. Joe Lewinsohn had offered to teach him law in the evenings until such time as he could pass the bar exam. Then they would form a firm of Auerbach and Lewisohn. The plan would be for him to get his share of the firm's money for the business he can throw their way and for the use of the Auerbach name. He would not be an "acting member" of the firm per se. He asked her advice and even suggested she might join him in studying law herself. Over and over, he expressed his confidence in their future together. "We're going to have a dandy time and we're going to work and we're going to make good, and before we get through, we'll make them all take their hats off to us."

In this spirit, Beatrice and George were married on April 5, 1911, at the St. Regis Hotel in New York. The evening ceremony, at 6:30 PM, was performed by Rev. Dr. Henry Ettleson, assistant rabbi of the Congregation Beth Israel in the city. Fannie was Beatrice's maid of honor, and Fred Auerbach served as best man. Beatrice wore "a gown of rare white silk trimmed with real point lace."[6]

Moses, Theresa, Fannie, and George and Beatrice before their wedding ceremony

After their marriage, Beatrice and George settled in Utah where both became active in the local community. George became a director in Walker Brothers Bank and was a vigorous supporter of a local newspaper and a baseball club.

In a tragic turn of events, Beatrice's first pregnancy ended in the birth of two stillborn daughters. Certainly that made Georgette's arrival in 1916 all the more joyous.

Not much is known about the Utah years, but probably the couple had an active social life. One attraction was the movie theaters in Salt Lake City. In 1912, barely a year after her arrival, the American Theater, boasting a seating capacity of one thousand, opened on Main Street amid considerable fanfare. "Audiences across the state delighted in the blunders of Charlie Chaplin and the Keystone Cops or thrilled at the sight of Indians attacking a wagon train and shootouts in the Old West."[7] Actually, as newspaper reporter W. Paul Reeve tells us, movie theaters were first established in converted storefronts along Main Street, even before the community was wired for electricity. One Charles Petty, store manager, ran the projector from a gasoline motor that created a loud *putt, putt* sound heard all over town; residents flocked to the venue in response.

A fledgling movie industry developed in Utah under the auspices of local entrepreneurs. The

Utah Theater Company and the Satchwa General Amusement Enterprises Company were among the earliest. Satchwa completed its first major film *Big Heart* in 1914. "A tale of Indian love and sacrifice, it premiered in Salt Lake City to rave reviews."[8] There can be little doubt that Beatrice and George were among the moviegoers. The Utah film industry was not to be long lasting; limited financing and remoteness from Hollywood and New York caused most companies to fail within a few years. But the enthusiasm for the medium never waned.

In his letters to Beatrice, George had referred to attending the services on High Holidays. When she arrived, most probably, Beatrice joined him at the Congregation B'nai Israel on the corner of Third South and First West streets. The synagogue was one of three in Salt Lake, each of which followed a different ritual. There was a Conservative congregation and an Orthodox synagogue as well as B'nai Israel, which followed the Reform ritual favored by most of the congregants of German descent.[8] But Beatrice made friends in the Mormon community as well, in particular, an elder of the Mormon Temple in Salt Lake City, who corresponded with her for several years, often sending along articles designed to uplift her spirit.

Life in Salt Lake City was neither glamorous nor easy. Much later, in 1944, Beatrice wrote to Georgette and Dick, recalling her experiences as a young mother in Salt Lake. In a letter to her mother, Georgette had recounted problems with diapering arrangements for young George, her firstborn. Beatrice responded, "It seems a long time ago (and actually it is) since I worried about problems like that, but I had them too. For the first nine months of your life, I had no nurse for you plus the fact that I lived in a little apartment." In order to give baby Georgette enough air, she said, she had to push her carriage up and down the street because "on the little side porch of the apartment, more coal dust blew in than anything else." She recalled too the difficulty of "hauling the baby carriage up and down the steps of the apartment." For a sophisticated Easterner, life in Utah must have had its share of hardships. But it would seem that George and Beatrice handled them well.

RETURN TO HARTFORD

A year after the fire, Moses Fox prevailed on Beatrice and George to leave Salt Lake City and come to Hartford where George could help him run the store. In 1917, Beatrice, George, and one-year-old Georgette arrived in Hartford where they moved into her parents' home at 534 Prospect Street. After staying there briefly, the young Auerbach family took up residence at 64 Highland Street in West Hartford. A second daughter, Dorothy, was born in 1919.

George went to work as secretary-treasurer of the store, and Beatrice, now with two daughters, led the life of a society wife. It was George who assumed the lion's share of responsibility for the construction of the new enlarged store. The building

Four generations: Hannah Stern, Theresa Stern Fox, Beatrice Fox Auerbach, Georgette Auerbach

was designed by New York architect Cass Gilbert. Initially, the eleven-story structure was dubbed as Fox's Folly in reference to its sheer scale.

George also became increasingly active in the community where he quickly earned a reputation as a civic-minded executive. Not only did he have a major position at the store, but he also was an incorporator of Hartford National Bank and a founding member of Tumblebrook Country

Club, a club established primarily for the Jewish community as a response to the exclusion of Jews by other Hartford clubs.

George also joined the Ararat Lodge of Masons where he met other area businessmen.[1]

Beatrice often spent time at the store, which enabled her to learn a good deal about the business. One intriguing item among the holdings of the Connecticut Historical Society is a textbook on accounting (*20th Century Bookkeeping and Accounting* by James W. Baker), which has Beatrice Auerbach's signature on the inside cover, and a number of notes that appear to be in her handwriting. The text was used at Huntsinger's Business School, which was in operation between 1917 and 1920. Most likely, Beatrice took a course at the school. At the same time, she assumed the duties of wife and mother. With most of the rest of Hartford housewives, she shopped for groceries at the Hartford Market and Pilgard's. At her height of five feet, reaching the top shelves was a challenge. In addition, Beatrice participated in civic activities during this period; for example, she was appointed as a delegate to the Conference on the Cause and Cure of War held in 1925 in Washington DC by the National Council of Jewish Women.

One organization of which Beatrice was a member was the Fifteen Club. On December 6, 1886, a group of women had banded together to form an organization named the Fifteen Club for the number of ladies present at the initial gathering. They determined that the club would be social and philanthropic and that dues would be paid to accomplish both ends. The existence of the Fifteen Club was of great importance to the unfortunate of Hartford's Jewish Community since it was established before the United Jewish Charities was organized. Members of the club visited poverty-stricken homes and patients at Hartford Hospital, the only hospital in the city at that time. It was exactly the sort of purpose Beatrice appreciated.

In the history of the organization, written in 1951, members are quoted as saying their "purses were always open" to those in need. So familiar were their charitable efforts that when the United Jewish Charities was formed in the 1930s, two members of the group were invited to attend their meetings.

Beatrice's mother, Theresa, joined the Fifteen Club and later brought Beatrice and her sister

Fannie into the fold. Both were staunch supporters of the charitable work done by the women, and Beatrice often hosted gatherings and, in time, sponsored both of her daughters, Georgette and Dorothy, for membership.

A close look at the minutes of the organization reveals frequent contributions to such causes as the Mile of Dimes (to combat polio), the Community Chest, the Cancer Society, the YWCA Around the World Fund, the Hartford Jewish Federation, the summer camps of both the *Hartford Times* and the *Hartford Courant* for children of the poor, and the Jewish Community Center Camp fund. A $100.00 life membership was purchased in the club's name in Mount Sinai Hospital. Often there were more specific expenditures listed, like "the purchase of shoes and rubbers for three poor boys," and occasionally there was mention of a "loan" to someone in need. The club also assisted World War II refugees.

The minutes sometimes reflected a lighter side of the group's meetings. On one occasion, the discussion turned to the merits of nylon stockings, a scarce commodity during the war years. At another time, after lunch at Tumblebrook Country

Club, the chef was asked for his recipes and advice on "how to keep a husband home" on the theory that a man's heart is reached best through the stomach. When meetings were held in the homes of the members, desserts became a focus for competition, several of the women bringing their best efforts to the gathering.

Further signs of the group's unconventional behaviors can be found in the minutes of several meetings. Reference is made to members "swiping" the floral centerpieces at the conclusion of a meeting; eschewing hats, thus flying in the face of convention; and serving Manhattans at lunch "in anticipation of the repeal of the Eighteenth Amendment."

At one meeting, Beatrice made a motion to establish a custom of sending a gift from the group to older members who were ill and unable to attend the gatherings. At the same meeting, she reported that she had been appointed to the Board of Directors of the Hebrew Union College in Cincinnati, most probably in recognition of her support of education and of a variety of Jewish causes.

Beatrice was proud of her Jewish heritage. She was an active member of Congregation Beth Israel, a reform temple of which her grandfather was a founder, and she attended services at the Farmington Avenue synagogue. Rabbi Abraham Feldman and his family were frequent guests at the Auerbach home. In the forefront of fund-raising for Jewish causes in the Greater Hartford community, Beatrice figured importantly in the fund drives for Mount Sinai Hospital and later the Hebrew Home for the Aged.

In 1925, the Auerbachs purchased a large brick house on Prospect Avenue from which one could see much of the city, including G. Fox & Company. The Auerbach home was magnificent. Designed by architects C. Grant La Farge and Benjamin Morris, the home had been built in 1911. When George and Beatrice moved in, they did some remodeling and engaged five persons to maintain the house and grounds. Gardener David Kidd developed the splendid terraced gardens, and Housekeeper Annie Bartels ruled the household with Germanic efficiency.

1040 Prospect Avenue

According to the *Hartford Monthly*, "The house served as a gathering place for national and international dignitaries. And the Auerbachs entertained lavishly. The sixteen-seat custom-designed Margolis dining table was a centerpiece for grand dinner parties."[2] Beatrice's chosen china pattern was the same as that used by the Danish Royal Family. Beatrice made certain that complete records of every menu be kept so that none would be repeated. After dinner, guests could enjoy their coffee across the foyer in the living room or out on the sunporch, furnished in black wicker. The sunporch offered a fine view of the gardens. One special sight was a sculpted figure for which the model was their nephew, Frederick Auerbach. The sunroom, located off the living room, was used more frequently during cooler months.[3]

In addition to their busy lives in the Hartford community, Beatrice and George shared an interest in agriculture. One Sunday, while out on a drive, George saw a For Sale sign on a property in Bloomfield. Shortly thereafter, he bought the working farm, which they named Auerfarm. The farm came complete with poultry, cows, and an apple orchard. George made several improvements to the property, and the Auerbachs were soon raising prize Guernsey cows. The family spent every summer at Auerfarm where they could relax the level of formality required of them the rest of the year.

In 1926, the Auerbach family took a trip abroad. George Auerbach kept a diary of the trip with his wife, his daughters, and a Ms. Tasker, their governess. The trip began on July 12, and the last entry in the diary is dated August 11. This may be the date of return, which would make sense if the trip was of a one-month duration, unless the diary is incomplete. More than likely, George needed to get back to work, and the girls would be due to return to school in a few weeks.

George and Beatrice at Auerfarm

They began the trip in England where they visited Warwick Castle, which impressed George for its massive size, the condition in which it was kept, and the magnificent grounds.

Visiting Stratford-on-Avon, George amused Beatrice with his recitation from the guidebook on Shakespeare's life. "He (Shakespeare) seems to have married Anne Hathaway in 1582. There were three children by the time Shakespeare went to London soon after his marriage." In Stratford, George asked their guide if the couple were happy. The guide replied, "Sure. He came back in 1596."

Though the trip was primarily a family vacation, George and Beatrice did contact a number of businesses with which G. Fox dealt.

Encountering poor food at the Regent Hotel, George complained to the waiter who responded, "I'm very sorry to hear it." George said, "That doesn't do me a bit of good." The waiter responded, "Oh no, sir, I did not mention it for that reason, but we waiters have to eat the same food as the guests."

In Glasgow, a waiter put his thumb in the soup while serving it. George refrained from chastising him because he believed he should act the gentleman when his wife was along. But he reports, "I did tell her, and she took 6p. off his tip."

In another entry, George remarked on the crisis in employment for men coming back to Great Britain from military service. In a particularly insightful note, he lamented the fact that public welfare offered more for a family of four than a man could earn working.

On one occasion in England, George and Beatrice struggled a bit with a bill of fare in French. Georgette asked, "Daddy, they always print the bill of fare in French here in England, don't they?" When he responded in the affirmative, she declared, "Then I'll be glad when we get to France because they will have to be just as polite and maybe they will print their bill of fare in English."

Suddenly, in 1927, George died under circumstances which caused Beatrice to lose trust in Hartford doctors for a time. A letter of referral dated April 27, 1928, from Dr. H. Gardner Russell in Hartford to Dr. Eugene Pool in New York explains why. "The deceased Mr. Auerbach having had a duodenal ulcer for several years before his death was under treatment in the Mayo Clinic and also in Hartford. The last flare-up being in early summer of 1927 when he bled severely. I saw him at this time regarding the question of transfusion. In the latter part of the summer, Mr. Auerbach was taken with sudden abdominal pain and a great deal of shock. After consultation, it was decided that his ulcer had ruptured, and he was operated upon within two hours. Operation disclosed no ulcer, and two hours after it's [*sic*] conclusion he had a similar attack and died. Autopsy disclosed a coronary thrombosis. Because of this mistake, Mrs. Auerbach has considerable feeling against the physicians and surgeons of Hartford . . ."

Newly widowed, Beatrice turned to working part-time with her father. Sitting at a desk adjacent to his, she began to learn the business. Theresa and Moses moved to 1040 Prospect Avenue sometime before the 1930 census, which lists them in residence there. According to Connecticut historian Robert Epstein, Beatrice "divided her time between her children and the store. She combined perfectly the role of business executive and homemaker. She was at her desk every morning, she lunched daily at home, and then returned to the office for the remainder of the afternoon."[4]

In January of 1932, Theresa Fox died, leaving Moses to become ever more dependent on Beatrice both at home and at work. Soon she became indispensable to the operation of the business and was second only to her father, and she continued working alongside Moses for eleven years, until his death on January 13, 1938. At that point, Beatrice became chief executive of G. Fox & Co. which, under her management, would become the largest family-owned department store in the nation.

FIRST LADY OF
THE EMPORIUM

"Elegant," "peerless," "immaculate," "beautiful," "inviting," "spectacular"— these and numerous other positive descriptors have come from everyone interviewed when speaking of G. Fox & Company. The epithet Center of Connecticut Living was clearly justified by all who knew the store and was the concept behind Beatrice Auerbach's management style. To put it succinctly, she worked to make G. Fox an extraordinary full-service department store that catered to the diverse community of which it was such an important part.

Mary Barry, a buyer for the preteen clothing department employed from 1947-1969, emphasized the significance of G. Fox to the city of Hartford and the state of Connecticut. Considering the development of the business from its modest beginnings to the eleven floors of rich and varied merchandise, one factor emerged as critical. In the case of Moses Fox and then Beatrice Auerbach, their constant presence and hands-on management policy ensured that nothing was wanting in the goods and services provided to the customer.

Many who recalled shopping in Fox's were effusive about the variety and abundance in the departments on every floor. Some could recite a litany of departments—main floor: jewelry, accessories, cosmetics, hosiery, handbags, umbrellas, liquor, and smoke shops; second floor: men's furnishings, Connecticut Room Restaurant, and the zipper repair department; third floor: blouses, budget coats and dresses, furs, sportswear, and maternity clothes; fourth floor: lingerie, housedresses, uniforms, yard goods, and the beauty salon; fifth floor: bridal salon, the speciality shop which featured designer clothes, millinery, gift shop, and a department devoted to artificial flowers; sixth floor: children's department, boy and girl scout shops, infant's wear, and nursery furniture; seventh floor: dinnerware, fine glass, china, silverware, and small appliances; eighth floor: drapery, curtains, and carpets; ninth floor: interior decorating, lamps, pictures and mirrors, television sets, radios and phonographs, the Beacon Hill Gallery which featured reproductions of eighteenth-century Boston furniture, and the Milling Road Shop which sold reproductions of eighteenth-century English furniture; tenth floor: bedding, furniture, a model house innovative for the time, and the infirmary; eleventh floor: Centinel Hill Hall and, of course, Toyland.

A visit to Toyland was a magical experience for generations of Connecticut youngsters who waited patiently in line to advise Santa of their Christmas wishes and to view a lavish display of playthings to delight the heart of any child. Especially exciting for the boys (and their fathers) was the remarkably large display of electric trains and accessories.

In Toyland, as elsewhere, everything possible was done to please the customer. Mike Peters, later to be mayor of the city of Hartford, worked after school during the Christmas holidays when he was sixteen years old. His job involved assembling items and then transporting them to the Talcott Street entrance of the store where customers, who wished to, could pick up their purchases. On one occasion, after assembling a bicycle, Mike stepped into the service elevator and elected to get on the bike while the lift descended. On the fifth floor, the doors opened, and facing him was Beatrice Auerbach. She inquired about what he was doing, and he responded that he was delivering a bike he had put together to the customer pick-up area. She said, "Very good. Now get off the bike!" While she had a good sense of fun, Beatrice held firmly to the notion that business is business.

4th Floor Lingerie Department
Walnut and cherry woods; yuba and avodire veneers

In his memoir, *Crossing Fifth Avenue to Bergdorf Goodman*, Ira Neimark confirmed the commitment to customer satisfaction.[1] Mrs. Auerbach had a reputation for demanding that each department carry enough variety of stock to anticipate the demands of any customer. Neimark recounted his experience when telling Mrs. Auerbach that he wanted to buy a harmonica for his five-year-old daughter Janie. Mrs. Auerbach asked the buyer to show them what he had in stock. He offered one for fifty cents and another with music for five dollars. "What do you have in between?" she asked. When he responded that these were the only two he had, Neimark recalled, "In a voice you could hear across the floor, BFA declared: 'I own this big store, but can never find what I want when I want it.'" Neimark confessed that he bought the 50-cent model "before she skinned the poor fellow alive." The incident spotlighted a position she took throughout the store, insisting that a basic item be available in a range of sizes, colors, and prices.[2] Mr. Neimark did hasten to qualify his remarks about the extent to which Mrs. Auerbach dressed down her staff. He said he did not wish to leave the impression that "BFA went around striking fear into the hearts of employees."[3] But she did demand that customers be provided with a range of choices.

A glance at the number and variety of departments illustrates the singularity of G. Fox. To be sure, there were other large stores in the city: Brown Thomson and Sage-Allen, for example, but neither held a candle to Fox's in terms of the range of goods for sale. On the mezzanine, one could find a book department with a rental library, photographic equipment and developing service, an optical department, and even a post office branch. In keeping with Fox's basic policy, "Everything for the benefit of the customer," a number of other special services were available such as interior decorating, shoeshine and repair department, fur storage and repair department, radio repair, custom gift wrapping, a sewing school, a travel bureau, and a hosiery repair department. The first pair of nylon stockings sold in this country was sold at G. Fox.

For several years, major names in the cosmetics and fashion fields would visit the G. Fox main floor and the women's fashion departments. The likes of Charles Revson, Estee Lauder, and Tobe Coburn were familiar presences to G. Fox customers.

In a 1947 address to the junior executive group of G. Fox, Mrs. Auerbach attempted to explain her management philosophy.[4]

We use the state map and the phrase "Connecticut Living" as our symbol. In it lies our past and future. To me it means that the people of Connecticut have certain living habits that are quite different, let us say, than the people of Georgia or Ohio. It means these living habits are reflected in the merchandise they will buy.

G. Fox & Co. is a sectional merchandising institution and therein lies its strength. This business is the purveyor for the 449,452 families who live in the 169 towns and on the 22,241 farms that make up Connecticut.

With respect to your suppliers, manufacturers, and other sources, treat and hold them as partners; tell them the wants of your customers, especially of items not available in normal markets. Ask them to share your burdens, your experiments, and the rewards that go with the solution of customer problems. Good relations with our resources are beyond appraisal.

Consider always that G. Fox is not only purchasing agent but host to Connecticut and as such must always be the gracious host—the host who anticipates the needs of his guests. Over the past hundred years, this store has tried to be alert to the living habits of Connecticut. When hundreds of families move to the shore for the summer, a fleet of delivery trucks immediately adds seventy-five shore points to their heavy schedule.

The important thing in the future is to consider every shopping habit that develops on the part of Connecticut people. It must be anticipated and made easier. When you find an important part of Connecticut coming to Hartford to shop in an atom-fired rocket—don't be surprised—get busy and provide them with the best rocket-landing field in the world and sell them better G. Fox & Co. atoms to power the rocket home again.

I see a glorious future for G. Fox & Company. Our fortunes will vary with the fortunes of Connecticut for we are an integral part of Connecticut Living. There isn't the slightest fear on my part of this store facing any kind of standardized nationwide merchandising formulas. Our strength will always lie in our individuality and awareness of Connecticut. Your children will know your customers' children, and when Connecticut has any need, together, we will anticipate it because we are Connecticut people.

She brought her notions about good business practices to others as well. Brooksie Koopman recalls attending an evening event in Hartford with her grandmother when she was about fourteen. Before the event, the two went to enjoy an early dinner at a Hartford restaurant, one of the few places to eat downtown at that time. They were seated in the center of the restaurant, and Beatrice looked around at the nearly empty room. After a few minutes assessing the situation, she called her waiter (who may have been the owner) over and spoke quietly with him, gesturing to the seats by the big front windows. She explained to him that he needed to seat his early guests by the windows so that passersby would look in and see people there and perhaps consider having dinner there too. The impression achieved would be that the restaurant was fuller than it actually was. Brooksie recalled that some discussion also involved strategically turning more lights on. "I, of course, was mortified by the whole thing, especially when we were moved to the table by the front window." Certainly Beatrice meant to improve the restaurant's business, but her interest in making Hartford an attractive place extended beyond her own environs. It went beyond Hartford, too, embracing all of Connecticut.

Such commitment is underscored in a letter addressed to the trustees of the New York, New Haven and Hartford Railroad dated September 9, 1938. She wrote,

"The lack of service which you are permitting in the operation of the Road from New York to Hartford is not only exasperating but, in the company's present condition, most deplorable.

"Hardly a week passes by when twenty to thirty or more of our staff do not make at least one daily round trip to New York. If there is any time at which adequate dining facilities should be offered, it certainly is on the 5:10 PM train out of New York.

"Last evening, with a number of our people, I was a passenger on that train. For a long time out of New York, the car was taxed to its capacity, and many could not be accommodated. When accommodations did become available, the service was immeasurably slow; and at a time when an order could be taken, about fifteen minutes before reaching New Haven, announcement was made that the car would be disconnected there. Any number of passengers expressed not only dissatisfaction, but disgust.

"Such operations on the part of the only railroad, which serves Hartford, certainly do not tend to encourage travel to this point. It would seem for the benefit of all concerned that this matter should receive your prompt attention, and that discontinuance of eating service should take into consideration the convenience of passengers rather than the convenience of the railroad.

"Unless this is done, we shall give consideration to other measures which will more suitably provide for the needs of those who travel for us and in our interests."

The letter, on company stationary, was signed, Beatrice Fox Auerbach, President.

Earl Elhart, in the 1938 issue of *The Executive Edition of Retailing*,[5] explored further the concept of Connecticut Living, which became a significant part of the G. Fox view of its customers. The idea was that customers who lived in Connecticut were close enough to New York to be influenced by its ideas, but they lived differently than their metropolitan neighbors. Elhart called it a lifestyle closer to English country living. "A well-dressed

New York woman may not have found it necessary to change her dress from morning until she dressed for dinner and perhaps she didn't even dress for dinner." Connecticut women, in his view, simply didn't live that way. According to him, the difference lay in the fact that a Connecticut woman met the same people more than once in a day. Her different activities demanded different outfits, and she spent more than half her life in her car.

G. Fox introduced the Connecticut Living concept to its customers, explaining the rationale behind it in keeping with Elhart's observations. "They live in Connecticut. They are not cramped into small apartments accessible to the subway. They don't have to commute on trains. They live in the country; their point of view is keyed to country living. They drive on country roads, they play golf without making a major expedition of it, they entertain each other at luncheon or dinner, they see a lot of their husbands. They have a grand time. They are living the kind of lives which are available to only the most favored New Yorkers. They already have what all the smart people of the metropolis are trying to get."[6]

In a special way, G. Fox had always recognized that its primary clientele were women. From the fancy goods shop established by its founder grew a wider appeal to female shoppers. As the author of one history observed, "Women of the early twentieth-century acquired newfound leisure time provided by labor-saving inventions. Unlike the old-fashioned store that one did not enter without a purpose, where merchandise was hidden in cupboards until the clerks brought it out, this new store offered many new services especially for women who now shopped as much for entertainment as for the accomplishment of an errand."[7]

When Beatrice took over the management of the store, she understood very well the need to market to women. She expanded the store and what it offered. Women could dine in a pleasant restaurant and have their hair done in a full-service beauty salon employing forty-five people. Lunch in the Connecticut Room might well include a fashion show with models touring the room wearing outfits featured in the speciality shop. At Beatrice's insistence, one of the models was always "mature," generally an attractive white-haired lady, to acknowledge the diversity of Fox's customer base. Various departments offered instruction to help women operate their new appliances with efficiency or design a tasteful interior. And the standard of service was exemplary. Each level of the store had a floorwalker who stood at a podium at the foot of the escalator and whose job it was to make sure things were operating smoothly on that floor.

On occasion, when a woman admired a dress in the window of the store, and learned one was not available in her size, a floorwalker would check the size of the dress on display and remove the dress from the window so that the customer could purchase what she wanted. It was standard practice to make the item on a manikin available to the customer. Though it is a rhetorical question, Ira Neimark asked, "Does anyone do this anymore?"[8] Beatrice Auerbach certainly made every effort to answer the needs of women while expanding the available goods well beyond apparel and the way it was used.

To handle orders that could not be processed easily by clerks in the various departments, G. Fox employed six personal shoppers. Typically, the shopper would select merchandise according to the details supplied by the customer. In many cases, the shoppers would develop files on their customers, including likes and dislikes, photographs and measurements; and often when customers visited the store, they would stop by to say hello to "their" shopper.

The personal shoppers also offered special services to customers in the store. According to Roger Dove, they would "conduct through the store blind persons, anyone who is handicapped or in a wheelchair . . . or a person who cannot speak English."[9]

Another free service extended to the shopping community was the help of a bridal consultant who handled a myriad of details today provided at considerable cost by a wedding planner. Of course, the service assisted in the selection of the wedding gown and the dresses of all female members of the wedding party. Advice was offered for the complete trousseau as well. Consultant Susan Drake described additional assistance, "We help in the selection of invitations. We register the silver, china, and crystal patterns . . . as an aid to relatives and friends who wish to purchase gifts. After the final fitting, wedding photos are taken in a private area of the bridal salon."[10]

The interior of the store itself bespoke its commitment to good taste and elegance: never ostentatious but always sophisticated. Visiting G. Fox was an aesthetic experience. Still cited as an excellent example of Art Deco style, the store was a model of dynamic design, with sweeping curves, glass counters, and marble floors. In the early '50s, a concave show window was added facing Main Street. Aluminum, stainless steel, lacquer, and inlaid wood were among the materials used in the structure and décor. And Mrs. Auerbach had installed on the main floor a number of Waterford chandeliers that she had personally purchased for the store. The effect was elegant, functional, and ultramodern.

For Beatrice Auerbach, service was the very essence of good retailing. She believed retailing was far more than merely a technique of getting people to part with cash. She once told a group of business students, "The true beauty of retailing is that it teaches people to like other people for what they really are. *Retailing* is a poor word," she said, "it is science and spirit and joy, the joy of working hard and the joy of thinking about other people."[11]

A host of stories developed around her devotion to her business. Her interest in the most-minute details was legendary. Beatrice would surprise the public and her employees by showing up amongst the bargain dresses, boxes, or other items. She was especially concerned with the appearance of each department, and she sometimes checked out the dressing rooms to see that no garments or hangars were left around after customers had tried on their selections. She established a great many practical rules too. For example, all receipts were written in ink except in handbags where the staff used pencil to avoid getting ink on a leather bag which then could not be sold.

She often wore white gloves while on her peregrinations around the store. More than one employee watched as she swept her hand over (and under) the counters, making sure that no dust was lurking unremoved.

The white glove, according to some recollections, housed an iron fist. Bennett Cerf, writing for the *Saturday Review of Literature* in 1947, recalled his first meeting with Mrs. Auerbach. Noting that she then owned and operated both G. Fox and Brown Thomson, he said, "Mrs. Auerbach brooks no opposition. She doesn't even recognize it. When she sails through her domain, even the steel girders tremble slightly. We all followed meekly in her wake, stopping especially to admire the spotless pharmaceutical department, which is patronized by the entire state of Connecticut. 'Here,' said Mrs. Auerbach, 'is a special machine for rolling pills. Push the left lever and a white pill drops out. Push the right lever and you get a brown one.' She pushed sharply on the right lever, and a white pill appeared! There was a moment of silence, and then someone said, 'Heads will roll for this. I saw the same thing happen in the Kremlin.'"[12]

In spite of her physical stature, Mrs. Auerbach was a formidable figure. This has been accounted for by some observers as a genuine charisma. Her public relations director said, "When she entered a room, you knew she was there at once."[13]

Coupled with her reputation for excellence, her personal charm made those meeting her for the first time a bit nervous. Bob Steele, a radio personality who would himself put Hartford on the broadcasting map with his morning program on WTIC,[14] recalled their first encounter. "I had a plaid suit. I looked pretty good," he said. Getting off the elevator, he was greeted by the woman herself. After complimenting him on his outfit, "she reached over, unbuttoned his jacket, and peered at the lining." She saw that the label inside did not say G. Fox & Company, and Steele said, "That was one of life's embarrassing moments."[15]

No doubt, his reaction was heightened by the fact that G. Fox was to be the major sponsor of his program, the *Morning Watch*. In fact WTIC was the major on-air carrier of the store's advertising. Not only did the store sponsor the *Morning Watch* from 7:00 to 9:00 AM, but it also presented the *Artistry of Homemaking*, broadcast directly from the linen and domestic department Monday through Saturday from 9:45 to 10:00 AM; *Fox's Minute Makeups* on Tuesday from 12:30 to 12:45; the *Story of Sight* on Thursday from 12:30 to 12:45; and *White Eagle*, thrilling tales of G-men sponsored by the Major Electric Appliance Department on the seventh floor, airing on Monday, Wednesday, and Friday from 7:45 to 8:00 AM during the *Morning Watch*. In its centennial year, G. Fox sponsored ten-minute radio vignettes called the *Highways and Byways of Connecticut* on WTIC. Each of these broadcasts highlighted one of the cities or towns of the state, underscoring the role of G. Fox as the Center of Connecticut Living.[16] The long association of G.

Fox and WTIC's *Morning Watch* began in 1937 and ended in 1973.

The exacting pride Beatrice took in her enterprise was matched by an unusual humility. In another pharmaceutical adventure, Frances Kaufman, a pharmacist at the Jefferson Street branch of G. Fox located in the Hartford Hospital Medical Building, recalled a particular day in the 1960s. Mrs. Auerbach, who occasionally visited the facility, stopped in, probably after a medical appointment. Fran was digging through the trash, trying to find a jar of ointment, which had on its label the prescription for a special formula and which had been inadvertently discarded. After warning her to be careful, Beatrice rolled up her sleeves and joined Fran in rummaging through the trash. They succeeded in finding the jar.[17] On another visit, she scrutinized the ladies' room to see if it needed any improvements, and later she had the nurses' lounge at the hospital redecorated.

Maurice Berins, longtime director of personnel, noted that, in spite of her tough manner at times, Beatrice rather liked it when someone stood up to her. "She didn't want you to agree just to please her." He praised her tough intelligence that could predict trends in retailing, keep exhaustive control of vast inventories, plan marketing campaigns and strategy. She didn't hesitate to call you on the carpet when she was displeased, "but then she would be so gracious the next time she saw you."[18]

G. Fox had an annual sale around Easter time. According to Ira Neimark, "BFA felt that the customers who bought from her all year round were entitled to a grand bargain at least once a year." She used this also as a motivating tool for her sales force. She created a contest between departments. "Each merchandise manager had sales goals for each department based on a percentage increase over the same period last year . . . Each day the sales people in the departments that beat the others received silver dollars with a fanfare of bugles. At the employees' entrance stood a large billboard which charted the status of each division in the competition."[19]

Beatrice believed that successful retail businesses are built with great sales people, not heavy advertising. Ira Neimark noted that "this emphasis on personalized and professional customer service has value that retailers today seem to have either forgotten or never recognized."[20] There are some who believe the commitment to service might have been taken too far. Eunice Kelly recalled that during the early years of the cold war, G. Fox, like most other businesses, had a plan to be followed in the event of a bomb alert. Simply stated, the policy was, "If the alarm goes off, you must complete your sale; then you may proceed to the subbasement."

In The *Grand Emporium*, Robert Hendrickson pointed out that G. Fox "had been one of the first stores to make home deliveries, and made them by wheelbarrow until the late nineteenth century when horse and wagon deliveries were started."[21] Roger Dove, in a series of newspaper articles about the store, wrote that in 1954, the fleet of 347 vehicles delivered more than two million packages. The blue vans were a common sight on the roads of Connecticut. Customers outside the state could have their orders sent by parcel post free of charge. Free express and freight shipments were made in Connecticut, Massachusetts, and Rhode Island as well. It was the only store in the country offering such delivery services gratis.[22]

Items purchased on December 24 were delivered that night by having the entire fleet of trucks make a second trip. Brooksie Koopman recalled accompanying her father, whose duties included supervising the delivery department, to watch the fleet of vans leaving the store on a snowy Christmas Eve in the mid-1960s. The trucks left in one long line after every one had been repacked with that day's purchases. A handful of service management executives and two or three drivers remained on duty, sometimes until after midnight, to dispatch replacements for gifts that had not been received in time to be placed under the tree for Christmas morning.

G. Fox was a major user of telephone technology. In order to handle telephone orders for merchandise, twenty-four operators staffed the switchboard full-time. Customers could call the store from any point in Connecticut toll-free, and the operator would connect them to an order taker.

In the 1950s, the store had active charge accounts in every state and customers on all the world's continents.[23] One New York customer expressed the attitude of many out-of-state clients, saying he used to live in the Hartford area and would rather shop at G. Fox by mail than in New York in person. A farmer in Maine swore by the store which, he said, never failed him, including the occasion when he ordered and received a set of snowshoes for his horse.[24]

A story was told of a New Haven woman who was moving her family to Indonesia. While she never visited the store, she ordered by mail and phone several huge fans, household items, clothing for her entire family, and enough fabric to outfit her household staff in Indonesia. The shipment was already on the dock when the family arrived in the Far East.[25]

Legends abound about the lengths to which G. Fox would go to serve its clientele. One account said that a truck was dispatched to deliver a single spool of thread. A similar tale claimed that one greeting card was delivered to a customer. For a time, some deliveries within the city limits were made by motorcycle. And occasionally, an employee would be asked to deliver a package to someone in his/her neighborhood on the way home from work. Such extraordinary service may well be seen as Beatrice's method of dealing with the competition from stores with suburban branches. So when R. H. Macy's opened a branch store in New Haven, G. Fox advertised the availability of same-day delivery service to New Haven, effectively blunting the new competition.

Ira Neimark recounted his experience on the way to his initial interview with Mrs. Auerbach. Driving from Providence, Rhode Island, he had a flat tire and was concerned that he would make a sorry impression by being late for the interview. Not five minutes after he stepped out of the car to fix the flat, a big blue delivery truck with the G. Fox logo stopped, and the driver asked if he could assist him. Grateful and amazed, Neimark told the driver he was on his way to a meeting with Mrs. Auerbach. The driver, he said, "acted as though he did this all the time." In retrospect, he says, knowing Beatrice, "it is possible she told her truck drivers to keep an eye out for a single driver with Rhode Island plates crossing the border at about ten o'clock. She was a very thorough lady."[26]

Ubiquitous as the blue and white vans were, in 1947, on the occasion of G. Fox's one hundredth anniversary, an extraordinary mode of delivery was put in place. According to executive James Elsner, a customer was identified in each of Connecticut's towns, and a representative of the store escorted that individual to a suitable open space in town where one of four helicopters hired for the purpose landed and the pilot stepped out with the expected package. Mr. Elsner was assigned the town of Washington, Connecticut, and he recalled the surprise and delight of the chosen patron.

The concept of pleasing the customer was manifested as well in the treatment of returned merchandise. Refunds were provided in virtually all cases with no questions asked. And if the customer requested it, a G. Fox van was sent to collect the item. The policy was practiced by her father before her. On one occasion, a woman wanted to receive credit for some sunfast curtains that had faded. The sales clerk approached Moses Fox to ask what to do since the drapes had been purchased fifteen years earlier. He asked her if the curtains had been sold as "sunfast," and she responded in the affirmative. "Well then," he said, "give her her money back."

One could return an item even without a receipt. For a long while, this policy worked satisfactorily; but when discount stores began to appear in Connecticut, people took advantage of it and probably returned items not purchased at G. Fox, receiving more money than they had paid for the merchandise.

Jane Keller Herzig, whose parents vacationed with Beatrice on Nantucket, told a story that points up Beatrice's awareness of the liberality of the return policy. One morning, Mrs. Keller and Mrs. Auerbach were walking along the beach when Beatrice bent down and picked up a toothbrush, which was in dismal condition. She turned to Mrs. Keller and said facetiously, "Do you think we should take this to Fox's for a refund?"

While Ira Neimark admired a great many of Beatrice's policies, he did cite a significant exception. All of the mail coming to G. Fox, addressed to anyone at any level, was opened and sent to her office. He discovered this about two weeks after joining the firm. "BFA called me to her office and handed me a large group of letters. Hiding my surprise was impossible. All mail addressed to G. Fox was company business, she asserted. If someone wanted to write to me personally, they should write to me at home. I politely labeled her business practice an invasion of privacy. She countered that such correspondence told her more about what was happening in her store than anyone could imagine. This practice of opening employees' mail was ultimately declared illegal. Who would have imagined that decades later, the same issue would arise with e-mail but with the reverse decision in terms of employees' rights?"[27]

THE CIRCUS FIRE

In 1944, the visiting Barnum and Bailey Circus was the scene of one of the most tragic fires in U.S. history. The circus had pitched its tents on Barbour Street, in the North End of Hartford. Every available seat for the matinee performance had been sold. The fire began as a small flame about twenty minutes into the show. The bandleader first spotted the flames and directed the band to play the "Stars and Stripes Forever," the tune that traditionally meant distress to all circus personnel. The ringmaster urged the audience to be calm and exit in an orderly fashion, but the public-address system failed, and panic ensued. Because the tent had been coated with 1,800 pounds of paraffin, commonly used for waterproofing at the time, the flames spread rapidly. The fiery tent collapsed in about eight minutes. Of the 7,500 to 8,000 people in the tent, 158 died; and hundreds were wounded, the majority of them women and children.

Beatrice immediately responded by sending five hundred sandwiches and twenty-five gallons of coffee to the Red Cross Mobile Canteen to keep workers and volunteers moving. The G. Fox vans were equipped as ambulances and used to clear the dead and the wounded. First-aiders and the store's four nurses were dispatched to the scene, and trucks delivered medicines to the hospitals.[1] "She heard there was a shortage of bedding and night clothes, so she sent over a truckload. Nurses opened the hospital linen cabinets to find brand-new sheets and pajamas, the G. Fox tags still attached."[2]

While the fire is remembered particularly for the lives lost and the many burn victims that survived with permanent scars, no one could be more aware than Beatrice Auerbach of the impact fire can have on individuals and a community. Twelve years later, in 1956, St. Joseph's Cathedral burned to the ground. Beatrice was one of the first to donate to the fund to rebuild the church.

ONWARD AND UPWARD

At the time of its one hundredth anniversary in 1947, G. Fox was the sixth largest department store in the nation and one of the handful of such stores with private ownership.

In 1938, with Beatrice Auerbach newly at the helm, the company had embarked on the third major renovation in the store's history. Before the excavation could begin for the erection of the addition, the Brown Thomson Building, which stood east of the store and which had been purchased by Moses Fox in 1934, had to be moved south as far as Temple Street. "Thus, an 8,000-ton structure was moved via steel rollers, and during the operation, all of the normal activities in the Brown Thomson store were carried on as usual. The task took only

**Celebrating the 100th Anniversary
of G. Fox and Company**

two days instead of the expected two weeks."[1] It was an engineering feat never before attempted in New England. Other daunting aspects of the move included the removal of sixteen thousand cubic yards of solid bedrock, twelve thousand cubic yards of earth, and the straightening of an angle on the old east building line where the old and new parts of the store were to be joined.

The eleven-story G. Fox building was expanded on every floor, one hundred feet to the east, to increase the selling space to forty thousand square feet. Escalators were installed from the basement to the eighth floor, and the entire building was air-conditioned. On a sizzling August day, one would shop first in Brown Thomson, where the hot air was simply circulated by fans, and then hasten over to Fox's with its pleasantly cool temperatures. Rena Koopman recalled her father telling her that electric eyes installed at the Main Street doors counted customers; charts were made of temperature versus number of customers, which showed the significant impact of air-conditioning on patronage on hot days.

Not everyone favored the expansion. In May of 1937, Beatrice received a letter from her brother-in-law Frederick in Salt Lake City. He wrote to urge her to rethink the expansion plans. Apparently Beatrice had recently fainted in New York and again in Mexico, though in the latter case the change in altitude might have been the reason. Frederick wrote, "I am disturbed over your physical condition and definitely feel that your spells are the beginning of heart trouble and unless you let up and not try to do three men's work that you will have a sudden attack just as I had, which will definitely incapacitate you if not terminate fatally." He urged her to go to a specialist for a thorough examination and cardiogram. "I am quite certain you will find that your heart has started to go back on you. You cannot abuse an organ like the heart, as you have done and are continuously doing, and not suffer the penalty."

Frederick knew her management style and was frank with her about why her approach to work was a source of concern in itself. "If you were of a nature that would decide to go ahead with a project and let others do the bulk of the work, it would not be so bad, but where you insist upon planning every detail, I think the proposed plans for the store and B.T.'s [Brown Thomson] are simply suicide for you."

He worried, further, that she was not being well advised, and he added his opinion that her father was no longer in a position to counsel her because he had come to depend on her and her legal advisor, Sol Elsner. Fred bolstered his argument by pointing to the political situation as a reason to proceed with great caution. "It looks to me as if we are definitely headed for a Fascism form of government, which I think will be upon us in a very few years; with it you will find the lot of the Jew becoming more difficult, and those Jews owning buildings etc., becoming the targets, just as they are in other countries. We definitely feel the Jewish question becoming a problem even in our own city The more inconspicuous Jews can hold their wealth, the more will they be able to retain." The overall economic picture did not look favorable to him either. He expressed the belief that there would be another market crash in the near future, and that it was "no time to burden yourself with too many loans or mortgages." Pulling out all the stops, he writes, "I am as certain as I am alive that were your mother alive, she would not sanction any such program as you contemplate." Fred's arguments notwithstanding, Beatrice went ahead with the renovation.

Beatrice Auerbach has been justly celebrated for her direction of the growth and success of the Hartford store. Certainly, it served as an inspirational model for retail establishments nationwide. Even more significant is the model her management offered with respect to personnel policies. As early as 1929, Moses Fox employed Maurice Berins as director of personnel. He reported first to Moses and later to Beatrice. A study of contemporary department stores cites only two that had a corporate officer for personnel between 1935 and 1950.[2]

Beatrice was quick to recognize that caring for her employees would yield the sort of loyalty that strengthens a business, and she made a number of moves to ensure that loyalty. In the 1938 expansion, the employee cafeteria was reequipped and air conditioned. Beatrice initiated a meals-at-cost program for employees and hired a French chef for the cafeteria. Meals were wholesome and featured fresh-baked goods and milk from Auerfarm. Where other stores had a single nurse available, G. Fox opened a seven-room infirmary in 1940, which had two dressing rooms, an examination room, a waiting room, and eight beds. Further evidence of attention to the health of the employees is found in a *Go-Getter* (G. Fox employees' in-house newsletter) of October 30, 1957, detailing a schedule for inoculations against influenza. Beatrice addressed her fellow employees, explaining the plan to immunize everyone. In part she wrote, "Being constantly concerned and interested in the welfare of its associates, your management offers to you, as soon as vaccine can be secured, immunization shots for the prevention of Asiatic flu, at no expense to you."

The *Go-Getter* itself provided a variety of features that underscored the family model of management and personnel. Any news about any employee's achievements or contributions was included. A list of birthdays and anniversaries appeared in every installment. And each issue contained a message from management, frequently written by Beatrice herself. Most issues were four pages long, but a special occasion, such as the annual Moses Fox Club dinner, called for the addition of a two-page insert. During the war, the *Go-Getter* was sent to all G. Fox employees who were in the armed services.

From 1948 through 1954, Eunice Kelly was the editor of the *Go-Getter*. She called Beatrice "the first power force I had ever known." That power was put to use for Eunice in a particularly delicate situation. It was Eunice's practice always to take her birthday off. Because her birthday fell on the day after a holiday one year, she assumed an exception would be made from the rule that to get paid for the holiday, one must work the day after the holiday. When she received her paycheck, she found that she had not been paid for the holiday or the day following it.

She registered a complaint with the timekeeper but was told she needed to speak to someone higher up. She followed a chain of command whose mantra was "rules are rules." Frustrated, Eunice called Mrs. Auerbach's office for an appointment. When asked what her business was, she replied, "I wish to discuss my birthday." Sure enough, during her meeting, she found Beatrice sympathetic to her plight. She picked up the phone and issued a simple directive: "Somebody pay this woman!"

The ability to call several hundred employees by name and her genuine interest in their personal lives—births, deaths, weddings, etc.—is legendary. In 1947, Beatrice established a tradition of special luncheons in the employee cafeteria. Invited to these were twelve to sixteen employees representing a wide range of responsibilities. The merchandise manager might be seated between the maintenance man and a bookkeeping clerk who was sitting beside a telephone operator, herself next to the buyer for children's clothing. Initially, Beatrice attended each of the luncheons, encouraging an interchange among the guests and ensuring that each person was recognized and asked for suggestions. The affairs came to be known as Mrs. A's Suggestion Box Lunches and later were referred to as the Family Circle. For her part, "Mrs. Auerbach shared plans for the store while reinforcing the importance of team effort and providing a forum for employees to discuss problems relevant to the business."[3] Suggestion boxes dotted the store, and every month prizes of $2.50 to $5.00 would be awarded for the best ideas. There was also an annual prize of $50.00 for the year's top suggestion.

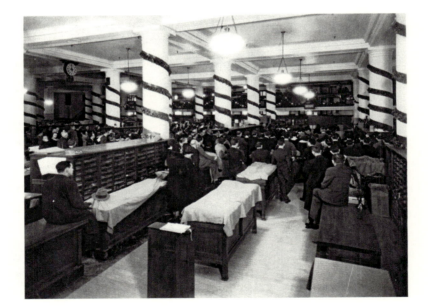

**Employees gather on the main floor of
G. Fox to hear Beatrice speak from Mezzanine**

Aware of the importance of employee recognition, Beatrice established the Moses Fox Club to honor veteran employees who had been with the store for twenty-five years or more. The club was launched with seventy-seven charter members in 1940. At the time, more than a quarter of the workforce had been with G. Fox for ten or more years, and much of this service came during the Depression, a period when no one lost their job at G. Fox. The newly created Connecticut Room Restaurant was the site for the initial event. Later on, as the number of longtime employees grew, the celebrations occurred in Centinel Hill Hall, an auditorium on the eleventh floor. These occasions were elegant and lavish, calling for formal evening dress. And the food and decor were of the highest quality. Beatrice presided at all of these gatherings and at induction presented each employee with a Revere ware bowl engraved with the Moses Fox Club name and the year.[4] Each year, a different gift was presented, such as a scissors and letter-opener set, a high-intensity study lamp, or a transistor radio.

The Moses Fox Club serves as an example of a practice common in American business in the first half of the twentieth century. The metaphor of a family of employees prevailed. In the case of another well-known Hartford firm, the Fuller Brush Co., members of their employees' club referred to the company founder as Dad Fuller. In all cases, these organizations bespoke a relationship between employer and employee that recognized the importance of each individual to the success of the enterprise. For G. Fox, of course, that loyalty existed well before the club, as exemplified in the maintenance of positions and the payment of salaries to G. Fox employees during the period immediately following the 1917 fire. It is a genuine loss to the world of business that the attitude of mutual respect and even affection between employer and employee is rare in the workplace of the twenty-first century. No one would have appreciated the magnitude of that change more than Beatrice Fox Auerbach.

While many of these policies were admirable, they were not exclusive to G. Fox. However, other innovations were unique. A case in point is the Theresa Fox Fund, a revolving no-interest loan fund for employee emergencies. Repayment schedules were based on the employee's ability to pay, and sometimes payments were as little as $1.00 a week. While this was a formally established fund, stories abound of Beatrice's personal generosity to employees in stressful situations. Hospital bills would be paid without the knowledge of the employee. A complete layette would be delivered to the home of one of her salespeople whose wife was expecting a baby.

Every year at Thanksgiving, Beatrice gave a bonus to each of her employees. All who had worked at least twenty hours per week for five or more years received a sum equivalent to one and one-half weeks' salary. One week's salary was given to those who had logged from one to three years at Fox's, and if the service was one-half year, the employee received one-half week's salary. Because Beatrice believed no one should go unrewarded, even employees who had been with G. Fox for less than one-half year found an extra $7.50 in their pay envelope.

In 1942, Beatrice took a bold step. She began to employ blacks in visible sales and management positions. One of these was Martha Taylor Shaw, a woman active in civic affairs and an expert on the minority subculture. She was hired to oversee the black employment initiative at the store. One day, Beatrice stepped into an elevator and greeted John

Stewart, the operator, who had frequently delivered her to her office suite. She said, "John, I like you. You're courteous. How would you like to join the sales staff in toys?" Over time, John Stewart became a supervisor, and he credited Beatrice Auerbach with "helping many of us get good jobs." Stewart later left G. Fox to become Hartford's first black fire chief. Local newspaper accounts credited G. Fox as the first in the country to hire blacks in anything but the lowest-level jobs.[5]

In order to ensure success for this pioneering effort, Beatrice asked Ms. Shaw to interview each department manager to make certain he/she was not racially prejudiced before a black employee joined the department. Eventually the screening was deemed unnecessary as blacks gained acceptance by proving themselves on the job. All of them were hired on an equal opportunity basis. In 1948, the G. Fox program was recognized by the National Urban League for its leadership as it set the example for other stores to follow.

A related activity, which absorbed her interest and energy, was the work of the North End Community Council. A majority of black residents lived in the North End of Hartford, and the council was established to make their voices heard. Following a meeting with them, she wrote, "After seeing what goes on, (I) can well understand that there is little conception of what the colored people have to contend with. To me conditions are just horrible and I really hope that I can be of some use in changing them. Most of the [committee] people are so smug and satisfied that it is going to take centuries before these people are going to have a fair chance."

Beatrice invited the director of the North End Community Center, Mr. Goodwin, to come into the store "to do some work with our own colored people. He feels it is necessary to separate the wheat from the chaff . . . . We have for selling now, one in stationery, in handkerchiefs, in children's, and in housewares." In signature fashion, she said, "I am naturally getting adverse criticism, but am going to carry on just the same." As a result of Mr. Goodwin's assessment, Beatrice met with two of her executives, Mr. Berins and Mr. Kyte. She wanted to clarify for them the issue of classes within the black community. Mr. Berins told her that "one of the difficulties we have in the store is that we do not discriminate between them with the result that we have those with poor background instead of good."

THE WAR YEARS

During the mid-1940s, Beatrice's first grandchild, George, was born in Texas. From the fall of 1944 through the summer of 1945, Beatrice sent weekly letters to Georgette and Dick. The correspondence reveals a good deal about her personal life and the life of the store during wartime. Few letters are without reference to employees and acquaintances serving in the armed forces. For example, she wrote, "We are having quite a few of the boys coming home. This morning one of the youngsters, who was a stock boy in the basement shoe department, came in. He has been in India two years and hospitalized because of ear trouble. Was a gunner and has worked his way up to Tech. Sgt. And is not quite twenty-one. He has developed into a swell kid who seems completely bewildered at being home, but is really some nice boy."

She had misgivings about how the military operates. Recounting a dinner with Herman Kaufman, one of the store managers home on leave, she wrote, "It just seems that the ways of the army are pretty queer when you think that his position was really an executive one here, and now his main duty seems to be changing bedpans and hanging around doing not much of anything—not being permitted to use his own initiative or his brain on any subject."

Women, too, were profoundly affected by the war. She herself had not seen her grandson. In December 1944, traveling by plane to New York City, she met a girl whose husband had a twelve-hour pass in New York. The young wife was to meet him at Penn Station but had no idea where and no sense of the size of the station. Beatrice and her chauffeur drove the young woman from the airport to the station, but she never learned if she found her husband or not.

The war had a significant impact on the store, both on personnel and merchandise. The Christmas season of 1944 found Beatrice at the end of her tether on both accounts. Her December 4 letter expressed her concern: "Today is supposed to be our big day in the store, and it is bedlam let loose with a crop of irresponsible people trying to do the job that really requires exquisite care. I am afraid that retailing under today's methods isn't a good go with me." The following week, she expressed even greater distress: "Saturday was one of those frightfully mobby days. The store broke all records in sales, but we also broke all records of bad service, and there isn't much satisfaction in doing things that way. They (the extra Christmas help) really are just terrible."

Although the seasonal business was booming, she wondered "how we do anything . . . as our stocks are so depleted, and in the lingerie department, I am not exaggerating when I say the shelves are actually bare, and the cry of 'Wolf! Wolf! No Merchandise' is really and truly on us now." One of the strategies employed in the face of the shortages was to stock shelves with empty boxes, providing a façade of ample supply. And she seemed on the edge of despair when she wrote, "Do you know I could not find even a broom in the store on Saturday?"

Beatrice did not forget the troops at Christmastime. In 1944, she informed Georgette that she had chosen to send "our boys," by which she meant those who left G. Fox to enter the service, a silver Dunhill lighter which, she believed, would please them. Her only regret was that there was no time to have each of them engraved.

In April of 1945, the country was stricken with grief over the death of President Roosevelt. "It really is a tragedy and one, I think, that everyone's going to feel," she wrote. Beatrice decided to close the store, and other downtown merchants followed suit. When word reached her of the president's passing, she directed that the G. Fox windows be immediately closed and draped with flags, and that no ads appear in the newspapers, devoting all space instead to tributes and memorials.

In June 1945, the troops began to return home, but not without controversy. "They are bringing a tremendous amount [sic] of boys from overseas back who arrive at Bradley Field. There has been a lot of ugly gossip to the effect that the boys have been smuggling in dope and diamonds." She bewailed the fact that this rumor had reached the newspapers, and that all returnees were being tarred with the same brush.

Ultimately, the issue of reassuming their roles in society created complexities for the veterans, their families, and the community. Always in the vanguard, Beatrice developed a plan "as a means of aiding former company employees to return to store service after leaving the armed forces, to train present employees in methods by which they can best assist such veterans in readjusting themselves to the latest retail practices, and to help both groups to become uniform in their dealings with the postwar public." She enlisted the help of the University of Connecticut, the Connecticut State Department of Education, and the Connecticut Reemployment Commission in the execution of the plan. The general postwar policy they designed became a model for other businesses across the state and the nation. The specifics of the policy were reported in the *Hartford Times* thusly: "The store will reinstate all former employees honorably discharged from military service; hire as many as feasible veterans interested in retail selling; endeavor to place as many handicapped veterans as will be practicable; prepare present store personnel to receive veterans as intelligently and with as much understanding as possible."[1]

A veteran of World War I, George Merritt of the personnel department was assigned to coordinate the program. He organized a series of four lectures, one each week, to provide necessary training for supervisors who would be carrying out the design. According to Mr. Merritt, "Present employees will have at their disposal all facilities of the program to aid them to find satisfactory answers for any question they may have in connection with veterans returning to their respective families, even though such veterans aren't store employees."[2]

Without question, Beatrice's correspondence revealed how the store responded to wartime issues. In one letter, she even urged Georgette to wait to buy war bonds until she was home and could get them through the store. Beatrice wrote, "The store's goal is past the halfway mark, but our quota is $1,006,815.00, so we are soliciting our friends and doing everything possible to attain that goal."

In her letters, she reported on her own activities at the time. True to her passion for the arts, she managed to see a handful of operas and plays between December 1944 and May of 1945. Among them were *La Gioconda* and *Norma* at the Met, neither of which she had ever before seen performed. She also expressed delight at Broadway productions of *The Song of Norway* and *Carousel* (which she called an operetta with excellent dancing). But the war was never far from her mind, as she declared in response to a musical called *The Seven Lively Arts* featuring Beatrice Lillie. Beatrice was distracted by the extravagant use of fabrics, which "added nothing to the cleverness of the show, but just represented bad taste and money and fabrics being used for nothing." She was thinking here about L85, a wartime restriction on the use of fabrics.

She did see a number of movies on trips to New York, and she especially enjoyed *National Velvet*, *Going My Way*, and *Meet Me in St. Louis*, which she dubbed "one of the best movies I have seen in a long time. It is gay, colorful, and not a war note in it. My idea of a real escapist's type of bliss."

Naturally, during these stressful times, friends and family did what they could to buoy up each other's spirits. She treated several people to dinner when in New York; a favorite restaurant was Voisin's. And at home, she had small dinner parties for family and a friend or two. The after-dinner ritual was to retire to the living room where they listened to Walter Winchell and played a long-running family gin game. Once she hosted a birthday party for family friend George Gershel. Seventeen guests were there for dinner, and she wrote, "George brought over a lot of dance records, and we took up the rug in the hall and had a merry time."

At the same time, she worried about the propriety of celebrating. On one occasion, for the 1944 Tobé Bosses' Dinner, an elegant affair, she was sent beautiful orchids to wear. She told Georgette she chose not to wear them, feeling that "orchids just at this time are anything but in keeping with the present mood." Others in her field did not have the same sensibility, as she made clear in her description of Coty's Annual American Fashion Critics Award Show at the Waldorf in February 1945. Twelve hundred very glamorous guests were treated to a lavish lunch. "It really was something out of this world and in my estimation completely alien to wartimes—but such is New York." Prizes

were awarded to designers Adrian and Tina Laser
and were presented by Mayor Fiorello LaGuardia.
Ever on the lookout for something to benefit G.
Fox, shortly after the event, she called Coty's Jean
Despres and asked to borrow some of the props
that had been used for the show, "so when we have
our own fashion show, I think we will be able to
add a little glamour at not too much expense."

The winter of 1944-1945 was an especially
severe one. Beatrice found herself hampered
by the weather a number of times. In January,
Beatrice was in New York for a business breakfast
after which she was offered a lift by sometime
journalist Alice Hughes. "Knowing it would be
completely impossible to get a taxi, I accepted
with great alacrity. When we got out on the street,
the snowplow had not been through Central Park
South, and Alice's car was just buried. I went to
one doorman after another, bribing them to the
extent of $5.00 so that they would get us out, as
of course Alice had no chains and no anything,
but not one of them would leave his post to come
to our rescue. Finally I spotted a man with a snow
shovel down the street and ran to borrow it, and if
you could have seen me shoveling out in the middle

of Fifty-ninth Street, you would have howled. I am certainly sorry that someone did not take a snapshot, as it would have been worthy of the *New Yorker*. Finally Alice got out, but the windshield was so completely frozen and ice-covered that she had to drive down Seventh Avenue with her head sticking out of the window in order to see. That is one experience I won't ever forget." And, indeed, it was memorialized in a brief article in the *Philadelphia Record*, a copy of which was sent to her by Henry Scherer, a family friend. The piece quoted Alice Hughes describing Beatrice as a heroine in time of need. According to Alice, the moral of the story was clear: "Always bring along a small, wealthy woman store owner when driving in a blizzard."

In February, Beatrice described the several feet of snow up to the library window. She continued, "The store business has nearly ground to a halt since only a skeleton crew can get there, and the customers are almost nonexistent." In her time at home, though, she kept busy. In a February letter, she said, "Tried yesterday to do something for the birds, but the most I seem to be able to do is to please the squirrels. I put some bread on the little iron balcony in large pieces, and wish you could have seen those squirrels carrying the whole thing away—when one came a whole lot of them put in an appearance and the little birds did not have a chance." She enlisted the help of her gardener, David, in devising a method to assist the birds and discourage the scavenging rodents.

Yet another winter-bred adventure occurred in late February. Her close friend Chase Woodhouse phoned Beatrice from downtown saying she had tried to get a taxi to come up to Prospect Street, but none was available. So Beatrice decided to come to her rescue. "Although I was dolled up in my lounging pajamas, I decided I would take my car out and go for her, as David wasn't home and Harry was off for the day, so down I went, opened the garage door and it was slippery as could be. (I) finally got my car out and started toward Terry Road. It happened that the ash man had been around to collect the ashes and had left the barrels in the driveway. Being too lazy to get out and remove them, I tried to drive around them with disastrous results, as I swung into a snow bank and there I stuck. Went back to the garage and got a snow shovel and the car started heaving, but to no avail. Of course, no one was there and I could not get up the hill, it was so slippery. Saw a light over at Jerry Kohn's and over I trotted. When they saw me at the door they almost passed out, especially in that outfit, with a scarf tied around my neck, rubber boots on my feet, and pajamas, but I hauled Jerry out to see what he could do. A newsboy came around at that time and we bribed him to do some shoveling, but nothing worked, so Jerry offered to take me down in his car and pick up Mrs. Woodhouse. We did this and finally got home, letting the car stay in the driveway all night."

In spite of the harsh winter, Beatrice continued to work on a number of causes in which she had particular interest. One of these was the Hartford Symphony Orchestra. An attempt was made by the two separate boards to merge the Hartford and New Haven symphonies. She wrote Georgette, "If both groups can forget their petty local difficulties, chances are something worthwhile will result" namely a really good Connecticut Symphony Orchestra. The merger was never to happen.

In January, too, in response to the relentless pleading of Dean Moshe Paranov, Beatrice pledged $5,000.00 to a fund drive for University of Hartford's Hartt School of Music; this was over and above the $1,000.00 already given annually to support the school's opera program.

Music was a constant in her life. In February, she wrote Georgette about a concert she had attended in Hartford featuring the violinist, Fritz Kriesler. "The house was overflowing with old-timers and along with them I am sure were the grandchildren, who were getting their first bit of musical education." She looked forward to the time when she would "be able to take little George in order to inculcate the proper interpretation that music can give to the unspoken feelings."

In the last week of April 1945, Beatrice began extensive dental work, which would dominate her life for several weeks. Her letters recorded her painful experience, but in spite of considerable discomfort, she soldiered on. At the beginning, she was directed to schedule a "forced vacation" during which she could have a number of visits with the dentist. For a month, she underwent painful procedures, telling Georgette in one letter that "the path between Dr. Hughes and my office shows more signs of wear than ever, and although they have adjusted and readjusted it, the extra paraphernalia in my mouth have affected the nerves in my head in a way that they have never before been affected . . . not to mention my digestive organs." Describing herself as "in the claws of the dentist," she urged Georgette to drink lots of milk to avoid her own fate with troubled teeth, a fate which, incidentally, was shared with her daughter Dorothy who had considerable trouble with her teeth. At length, in June, Beatrice reported that she was disciplining herself in the use of her "choppers," but "either I am very inept, or have a very peculiar mouth . . ."

In 1944, G. Fox initiated a five-day workweek. The store was open Tuesday through Saturday and Thursday evening. Apparently Beatrice persuaded other Hartford merchants to follow her lead, providing consistent work schedules for all of the city's retail establishments. This move ensured that all key personnel would be in the store during open hours, and it also enabled G. Fox to effectively compete for qualified personnel with Hartford's many insurance companies.

Each employee was granted a twenty-minute afternoon break and a half-hour free one day per week to do personal shopping. G. Fox had a scholarship program for children of employees.

The store instituted a noncontributory retirement plan and postretirement medical checkups for veteran employees, including arrangements for hospitalization when necessary. The plan was one of the first of its kind in this country.

Opportunities for women to advance were many, and it goes without saying that a woman at the helm fostered the success of others. Looking from the vantage point of the twenty-first century, the role of Beatrice Fox Auerbach in the advancement of women is remarkable. In fact, the term *protofeminist* is justified to describe her contributions to what was to become popularly known as the feminist movement in the 1960s. From the time that she assumed the presidency of the store in 1938, she worked in several ways to improve opportunities for women. In the store itself, a number of positions of responsibility were held by women, and promotions were as common for women as for men.

In 1939, as a means to bring more women into important positions in retailing, Beatrice established a major in retailing and allied arts at Connecticut College for Women. Initially, the program was directed by Florence Harrison and later by Chase Woodhouse, professor of economics and a close friend. An important component of the major was a six-week internship at the store in the summertime. Janet Harmon, a member of the first group of apprentices, described her experience as a total immersion in the organization and activity of the retail establishment. Interns spent time in every department and learned every phase of the operation. While in the program, the group lived together, dormitory style, occupying a floor of the Heublein Hotel. Phyllis Katz, who was an Auerbach intern, recalled the singular exposure she had to the inner workings of G. Fox. Both women used the term *mentor* to describe Mrs. Auerbach. Beatrice was directly involved, in her customary fashion, in making the program an effective and successful education experience.

The August 17, 1951, issue of the *Go-Getter* focused on the details of the Auerbach major. "The girls selected are in no way obligated to return to G. Fox after graduation or to enter the field of retailing at all." Nevertheless, retailing became the number one choice of most of the more than 125 graduates of the program from its inception in 1939. In the first year as an intern, the young woman became familiar with all of the operations of the store. During her second year, she devoted her time entirely to research projects from which both the individual and the store would benefit. One Auerbach major, for example, did a survey of Customer Lists used in each department.

No doubt, Beatrice's most significant effort to educate and advance women was the creation in 1945 of the Beatrice Fox Auerbach Service Bureau for Women's Organizations.

THE SERVICE BUREAU

In a 1965 *New York Times* interview with Leonard Sloane, Beatrice said, "My greatest interest has been human beings. I was always motivated by the human angle." Nowhere was this better illustrated than in the Service Bureau for Women's Organizations, which was supported by the Beatrice Fox Auerbach Foundation with an initial gift of $6 million.[1]

For two years prior to the bureau's initiation, Beatrice had been seeking a vehicle through which she could benefit the community and, in particular, women. After consulting with state leaders, she established a statewide nonprofit education service dedicated to assisting voluntary organizations in planning and executing their own programs and in developing among their members "leadership, perception, and understanding in areas of their interests."

She clearly articulated her goals in a pamphlet: "The volunteer's role in society has become increasingly complex and vital to the nation. Americans today are active in virtually every field of human effort. The Service Bureau, in cooperation with voluntary organizations, seeks to present educational opportunities for men and women to develop their ability as leaders, to extend the horizons of their knowledge and to acquire a fuller measure of understanding of the world around us."[2]

The bureau was born in 1945 and grew year by year until its aims were reached by several distinct groups. Run by a director and a staff of eight, the bureau, with a committee of advisers outstanding for their knowledge of voluntary organizations and their civic activity, formulated programs to serve the interests of member organizations who used the advisers to assist in locating, encouraging, informing, and training new leaders at all levels among the women of Connecticut.

To belong to the Service Bureau, an organization had to be voluntary, with a national affiliation, and at least five local chapters in Connecticut, with a broad educational purpose. Initially, seventeen groups affiliated with the Service Bureau.

In brief, the Service Bureau's was not a program competing for attention with other women's organizations, but it was one which would implement their programs and make them more effective. It offered two major series each winter in Hartford. One series included three meetings on education, and the other held three on international affairs. Each June, an all-day conference in each of three centers in Connecticut featured courses in organization techniques, such as leadership training, parliamentary law, public speaking, program planning, and public relations.

One of the early services developed by the bureau was a resource center that provided an extensive collection of current pamphlets, periodicals, and books on education, community affairs, and international relations. The education aspect of the Service Bureau quickly established two diverse strains. The first was manifested in a series of workshops designed to train women for leadership roles in their organization. A regularly recurring set of topics included Handling the Press, Fundamentals of Group Discussion, Hints for Program Planners, and Organizational Training.

Beatrice's own youthful travels with her family inspired her to educate women and their organizations on international issues. This effort to develop global awareness and perspective on international citizenship was of great personal interest to Beatrice. "Travel with my parents had a broadening influence on me as a human being and more than anything else gave me insight into the oneness of the peoples of the world," she stated. "Regardless of race, color, religion, traditions, or background, they all had one thing in common, the need for one another. The concept of service to others began to develop in my subconscious." Later, she said, it became clear in her retailing experience that "it is the selling of service rather than products that is important . . . the filling of needs rather than the selling of merchandise."[3]

Two early developments in international awareness were a "Welcome to Connecticut" program for international students attending Connecticut's private and public colleges and group visits for women to the United Nations.

The "Welcome to Connecticut" program brought together students from many countries who gathered for a primarily social event in the early fall of each year. This event was held in G. Fox's Centinel Hill Hall. One program for the event included a welcoming salute by Beatrice, an introduction to the Nutmeg State by Ward Duffy, editor of the *Hartford Times*, a talk on first impressions of the United States by a Japanese student at Yale and an introduction of women serving as hostesses to the students for the duration of their stay in the United States. The program was followed by refreshments and dancing with entertainment by Yale's Whiffenpoofs. The welcoming program became an annual event on the bureau's calendar.

Visits to the United Nations were initiated because Beatrice recognized the need for citizens to know more about that organization. In a communiqué, Ursula Duffus of the State Department division of organization activities expressed shock that "the combined efforts of official and private agencies to inform the people of this country about the work of the United Nations and, in particular, the economic and social side of its work have been pitifully ineffective or inadequate, or both." Ms. Duffus remarked about meetings of three groups of above-average educational attainment and organizational contacts and observed that "they had practically no conception of the economic and social problems which need to be tackled as a part of an effort for international peace and security, not to mention having practically no conception of the machinery of the United Nations set up to work on these problems." The inadequacy of press coverage was also obvious to her.

On January 20, 1947, to strengthen knowledge about the UN, Eleanor Roosevelt spoke for the Service Bureau in Centinel Hill Hall. She had just returned from the third assembly of the UN at Paris. Known throughout the world as ambassador without portfolio, Mrs. Roosevelt engaged the audience in a lively question-and-answer session following her remarks. She emphasized the role of the UN in keeping peace and creating an atmosphere wherein peace can grow, stressing the real advances she felt had been made by the World Health Organization, the Economic and Social Council, and groups assigned to seek out and reduce causes of war.

According to Mrs. Roosevelt, "The influence of women in maintaining world peace is a tremendous factor . . . because they have a desire to crusade for peace . . . . Unlike the men of most nations, they are not trained to believe war is inevitable." She believed women would "guard against aggressive tendencies by a military force assembled for defense" and "remove some of the causes for war—prejudices and age-old habits of thought." She asserted that she had "never heard one dissenting voice among women working for peace," even if compromise and sacrifice were necessary to achieve it.[4]

Picking up on Mrs. Roosevelt's encouragement, the Service Bureau made the UN visit a regular occurrence. Three or four times each year, a group of women from the various member organizations toured the UN in New York City and visited with representatives of various nations, and Beatrice continued on her own part sharing details of her experiences traveling all over the world. Some of the trips on which she reported were her trip to Africa in 1953, which included visits in French Equatorial Africa, Belgian Congo, Kenya, the Gold Coast, South Africa, and her visit to Europe in 1956, in particular the major cities in Russia and

Poland. In 1957, she visited Asia. Included in this trip were stops in Rangoon, the Philippines, Burma, Bangkok, Malaya, Bali, Java, Singapore, Saigon, Hong Kong, Taiwan, and Tokyo; and in 1958, she visited Australia and the Middle East. This trip featured stops in Lebanon, Karachi, New Delhi, Calcutta, Darwin and Sydney, Australia, New Zealand, Fiji, Samoa, and New Guinea. In 1959, the destination was South America where she visited Brazil, Argentina, Ecuador, Chile, Paraguay, Bolivia, Peru, and Uruguay. Her detailed travel diaries are a great source of information about the state of the world at the time of her visits.

A cursory examination of the annual themes on which programs of the Service Bureau were developed revealed how significant the work of the bureau was, and how very forward-looking were its concerns. In 1950, the theme was the American Woman as Breadwinner, Homemaker, Citizen. In 1952, the bureau examined preschool education and in 1953 the role of guidance counselors. In 1954, attention was turned toward the problem of homeless men. And in 1958, the focus was on the older years, including discussion of the United Auto Workers' Handbook on Retired Workers.

One of the most comprehensive and important contributions of the Service Bureau came in their publication of three studies on children and the law. The major work of the three was a 367-page compilation of the varied Connecticut and federal statutes affecting troubled children. Called the *Legal Rights of Children*, the study placed these laws in rational order within a framework of explanatory text that made the law comprehensible to lawyer and layman alike. Regulations governing abused and neglected children, delinquent children, and children in need of supervision outside their home were all included.

Many in the legal community deemed this compilation to be a valuable addition to a lawyer's research library. Of particular help, they felt, was the explanation of legal and judicial procedures. In a chapter on the juvenile court, for instance, a lawyer or layman dealing with a juvenile offense for the first time could find a step-by-step guide to the juvenile court process interwoven with text and comments by court officials that clarified the process.

A second handbook was called *The Police and Children in Trouble*. It gave police officers the proper procedures to follow in handling children when they are encountered in family emergencies, suspected of crimes, or are found in situations of abuse or neglect. The rights of the children and the police were clearly delineated.

The third publication, *School Law*, was a handbook for teachers and school administrators. All statutes pertaining to custody, control, and care of children in school were set out in readable and informative text, followed by a series of answers to questions they might raise.

The legal community honored the Service Bureau for its contribution in bringing clarity and order to a broad field of law. As something of an outgrowth of this work, the Auerbach Foundation funded a pilot project to develop a law-related curriculum in the Norwich, Connecticut, school system. Included in the elementary curriculum were practical issues in law that might apply to the young, such as school vandalism, shoplifting, loitering, abuse of postal laws, and illegal use of the telephone.

From its inception in 1945 through the late 1960s, Beatrice was not only the guiding spirit and chief supporter of the bureau, but she was also among its most active contributors. She opened her home on Prospect Avenue to a number of social gatherings entertaining the bureau's distinguished and celebrated guest speakers. Typically twelve to eighteen guests, assembled because of their interest in the field of the speaker, attended a dinner party.

A list of some of the guests of honor testifies to the wide range of fields engaging the Service Bureau. Politicians included Lowell Weicker, Abraham Ribicoff, Chester Bowles, Dean Rusk, Raymond Baldwin, and Ella Grasso. Among educators were university presidents Homer Babbidge of UConn, Kingman Brewster of Yale, and Harvard's James B. Conant. Writers John Hersey and Lillian Galbraith were included, as were performers Lillian Gish, Gloria Swanson, and Zsa Zsa Gabor. World figures in whose honor Beatrice hosted a dinner included Howard University professor of political science and Nobel Peace Prize recipient Dr. Ralph Bunche, Swedish diplomat and Nobel Prize winner Alva Myrdal, Admiral Chester Nimitz, and Eleanor Roosevelt.

Each summer, Beatrice hosted a picnic at Auerfarm where women representing the major

Service Bureau member organizations could gather in a relaxed setting to share their insights and ideas. One invitee expressed pleasure at the thought of a swim after luncheon. The splendid swimming pool at the farm was exceptional for its time.

While the atmosphere was casual, the conversation was decidedly focused. In discussing plans for a workshop on conservation, emphasizing clean air, they talked about what legislation had been achieved, what further legislation was needed, and how the women could help implement it.

After attending a picnic in August of 1955, Mary Sheridan, head of the Connecticut Division of the American Association of University Women, wrote to Beatrice: "Though I have read several times the excellent accounts from the *Hartford Times*, I have not had an opportunity to write you about them. They are thrilling." She went on to say, "You never seem rushed or preoccupied, and yet you accomplish. What you accomplish is not limited, sentimental, or vague. It is actual, constructive, and farsighted. And you have also carried through the responsibilities of a home, children, and ten strong, happy-looking grandchildren."

"MRS. A" AT WORK

In the case of Beatrice Fox Auerbach, separating the woman from the enterprise is difficult if not impossible. Her imprint is found on every phase of the business, and we can learn much about her values and her personality by examining her work life.

Describing her management style, the term *micromanager* seems eminently applicable. On a typical day, Beatrice would breakfast with her family, and because his age made it difficult for Moses, she would shave her father before leaving the house. She would arrive at her eleventh-floor office suite in the Main Street store at about 9:30 AM. Her personal hairdresser was waiting for her and would arrange her long hair into an attractive updo.

Beatrice at her desk

This ritual was followed by morning meetings with members of her staff, buyers, and managers. Lunch was incorporated into each day's business. Guests would be invited to join her in her office or in the store's Connecticut Room Restaurant.

In the afternoon, Beatrice toured the store, making certain that an abundance of goods was always available, and that customer service was paramount. One way in which Mrs. Auerbach monitored the departmental operations was to review the "want slips" prior to her daily tour of the store. Want slips were customer requests for unstocked or out-of-stock merchandise. She would also ask to have each department send their customer special order files to her office once a month.

She insisted that each department maintain basic stock books, which showed the number of units required to be on hand in order to serve customers properly. "To be out of a basic item was heresy, and treated accordingly."[1] At about five forty-five, she returned to her office where she received and reviewed the day's sales figures department by department. Ira Neimark recalls her telling him, "My store would still be small if I didn't watch all the details." A Manhattan cocktail was always ready for her at the conclusion of the workday, and she left the store each day between 6:00 and 7:00 PM.

The routine prevailed with the frequent exception of Mondays on which her chauffeur drove her to New York City where she had an apartment at 17 West Fifty-fourth Street, overlooking the sculpture garden of the Museum of Modern Art. As a season ticket holder at the Metropolitan Opera, she rarely missed a production. Often she dined with her sister Fan and Fan's husband, Les, who would attend the opera with her. At times when she was not attending the opera, she frequently took in symphony performances. Music always was a very important part of her life. Occasionally she remained in New York City to do business on a Tuesday, but most often, she was back in the Main Street store conducting business as usual.

When asked to describe Mrs. Auerbach, those who were employed by her for a number of years used adjectives such as *assertive, immovable, demanding, cordial*, and *fair*. One such employee was Trudi Lovell, who worked in accounts payable at G. Fox from 1948-1982. Three or four years after she began at Fox's, she lost her beloved father. Devastated, Trudi asked for a month off to settle the estate and to cope with her loss, made all the more difficult because both were survivors of the Holocaust. While the request for time was granted, Trudi had no expectation of salary during her absence. A large basket of fruit arrived at Trudi's home the day after her father's death. And each week, for four weeks, a check for $100.00 came in the mail from Mrs. Auerbach. In later years, knowing of Trudi's love of music, Beatrice would often pass on to her concert tickets she was unable to use herself.

When news reached Beatrice about one of her employees whose son was to be ordained into the LaSalette priesthood in Rome, an event that his mother could not afford to attend, she supplied the airline ticket that allowed the woman to be present at the ceremony. Examples of such private charity toward employees are legion. And news of them spread through the workforce so that not only the recipients but also most of the employees grew in admiration for and loyalty to their generous employer.

To respond to employees with special needs, two funds were established. The Moses Fox Fund was administered by local hospitals, and medical expenses for employees were often paid by this fund at a time when medical insurance was not yet a common benefit. In a series of letters to Dr. I. S. Geetter, head of Mount Sinai Hospital, Beatrice reviewed the terms under which her father had established the Moses Fox Free Bed Fund with a $10,000.00 endowment. A provision of the agreement allowed the Fox daughters to designate the user of a ward bed and free treatment for 200 days each year. Beatrice pointed out that it had been their practice to give preference to those associated with G. Fox & Company. An additional Moses Fox Free Bed Fund was established at St. Francis Hospital and was underwritten by Mrs. Auerbach. The terms were similar, but the coverage was extended to 365 days of treatment. When there was a shortfall in the cost of providing service in 1947, Beatrice wrote a check for $215.81 so that the hospital would suffer no loss.

Later on, G. Fox was one of the first companies to provide medical coverage to its employees. The lion's share of the credit for accomplishing this goes to her son-in-law Richard Koopman. A second fund, mentioned earlier, was named for her mother, Theresa Fox, and was maintained at the store to provide interest-free loans to employees who had serious need of them.

An important concomitant of the family image was the all-for-one and one-for-all climate established by it. Personnel Director Maurice Berins said, "People had job security. They knew they wouldn't be fired without being given every chance to improve. Training was going on all the time. Today, managers aren't willing to pay the extra money for that, to devote the time to it that it takes . . . most important, people knew we had a policy of promoting from within, that if they would just be patient, they would rise through the ranks." [2]

Even when an employee left the staff, Beatrice frequently conducted a personal interview to determine the reason for the departure. Beatrice Kramer told the story of her visit with Mrs. Auerbach in 1948. A single woman, Ms. Kramer explained that her social life, which had been very active when the USO was operating in Hartford during World War II, had become almost dormant in the postwar period. She told Mrs. Auerbach that she was moving to California to seek a livelier social scene. While Mrs. Auerbach expressed disappointment at losing a valuable worker, she also offered good wishes and some motherly advice. And she gave Ms. Kramer a parting gift, in this case a leather purse. These exit interviews happened often enough to be described as policy.

In January of 1947, Beatrice was presented with the Tobé award for distinguished contributions to American retailing. The award, established in 1942 by Tobé, the influential head of a New York firm of fashion consultants, was designed to recognize outstanding leaders in the worlds of fashion, commerce, and public affairs. The fifth person to receive the award, Beatrice, addressed her remarks to the audience, noting that she considered her position "a heritage, a partnership, and a trusteeship."[3]

A number of prominent retailers, educators, public figures, and members of the press were on hand to celebrate with Beatrice. Introducing her and congratulating her on behalf of her home state was Governor James McConaughy, who observed that he was the only man present who could claim to having purchased every item he was wearing from her store. Presenting her with the award, Adam Gimbel, president of Sax Fifth Avenue, said that one of the strongest factors in the committee's decision was Mrs. Auerbach's "extracurricular activities." In addition to establishing her retailing major at Connecticut College for Women, the Beatrice Fox Auerbach Foundation, and the Service Bureau for Women's Organizations, the trustees had noted that Mrs. Auerbach was "vitally interested in all communal affairs and was known throughout Connecticut for her many philanthropies." The text of her acceptance speech corroborates the committee's perceptions and offers an insight into her approach to her role as a retailing executive and a citizen of her community.

Beatrice receives the Tobé Award
Left to right: Adam Gimbel, Beatrice,
Connecticut Governor James McConaughy

After expressing her thanks for the award, Beatrice addressed her audience:

Whatever I may have done to be named for this distinction is not mine alone. It is but part of a heritage from the past, a partnership with the present, and a trusteeship for the future.

The year 1947, as has been explained so graciously, meant much to me in marking the one hundredth anniversary of G. Fox and Company. The store was founded by my grandfather and for fifty-eight years directed by my father. From them, and from the tradition of New England, I, as the third generation, learned the values of steadfast principles in life and in work. This is my heritage.

I know that no one's work is done alone. It is extended on every front by the creative talents and devoted efforts of one's associates, from the highest to the humblest. It is they who carry out the activities of an institution day by day, and their energies, fused with one's own, forge an institutional character as distinctive as human character. This is my partnership.

Coming from a part of America that is no longer young, I regard my own direction of G. Fox and Company as but a chapter in its history, and the store itself as a public servant of the community, the people of Connecticut. This is my trusteeship.

But none of these are static things.

In an activity as alive as retailing, each moment brings its challenge, and each must have its response. To define the challenge and create the response is our responsibility.

I see a challenge in the year ahead to all of us who are in the business of distribution. That challenge is to help stretch the purchasing power of the American family, by offering the best possible values in the best available qualities of the most essential merchandise.

It is very well to use the economist's language and say that in a period of high prices, if you can keep up unit sales, dollar volume will take care of itself.

But unit sales are only the total of all the purchases of American families for things in stores after they have carefully counted the family earnings and spent what is necessary for shelter, food, health, education, and recreation.

My own concern during 1948 will be to see that the people of Connecticut get the most of that which is essential to their needs and welfare.

This is a great challenge, and the response will be to make every endeavor and bend every effort, to strengthen their sense of security and be worthy of their confidence, by going back to first principles in buying, promoting and selling Good Values.

I am honored to accept the Tobé Award for 1947, and may its giver be blessed with health and strength to continue to share herself with us through the years ahead, and may she find joy in the knowledge of our appreciation.

While the speech itself reflected a number of the reasons why Beatrice was such a singular person in her field and in her state, the congratulatory wires and letters sent to her on the occasion pointed even more specifically to her position in the community.

Ethel Austin of Hartford wrote, "I think that women are always glad when another woman accomplishes an outstanding feat—for there is no doubt that even with the progress made, women still have a fight to reach the high places. Every time one of us reaches another peak, it is a step for all of us, and this is not the first time that all women in retailing will have cause to thank you for the achievements which in gaining for yourself you have in turn gained for all of us . . . . I am particularly glad the award was given to you for community interests for it helps to explode the myth that women in business haven't time for any other life. It proves that we can work hard and still be a force for good at home."

Rabbi Morris Silverman of Hartford's Emmanuel Synagogue wrote, "Fox's Store is more than a commercial institution! Through your vision and initiative, Fox's Store plays an important part in promoting the well-being of our community . . . . As deputy chairman of the Connecticut Interracial Commission, I know the splendid work you are doing to give colored people equal opportunities of employment. May your example of civic responsibility and true brotherhood be emulated by other individuals and institutions."

Deputy Commissioner of Welfare for the State of Connecticut Marjorie G. Siskey paid particular attention to Mrs. Auerbach's leadership of the Service Bureau for Women. "Your efforts to coordinate and give purpose to the women's organizations in Connecticut, particularly in movements pertaining to the welfare of children, have been of great value to us. Many persons have spoken of the benefits they have received through being given an opportunity to participate in these programs. Other states have expressed their interest and are hoping to pattern a comparable program."

And Edward J. Hickey, commissioner of state police, was probably the most eloquent of all in his congratulatory letter. He wrote, "You have indeed richly deserved this honor. The present impressive department store of G. Fox & Company, Inc., is a far cry from the tiny store of Gershon Fox, your grandfather, which sold shawls, ribbons, and laces. And yet, the same friendly service characterizes your larger establishment, and your patrons receive the same consideration and courteous treatment accorded to his customers a century ago.

"I have watched the phenomenal growth of G. Fox and Company with great interest. I have seen the present great store rise Phoenix-like from the ashes of the store that went up in flames on January 29, 1917. This remarkable expansion has been no mere accident—it has been your personal supervision and vision. Yours has been the hand guiding the destiny of one of America's most outstanding stores. Your personal and sympathetic interest in your numerous employees—your many innovations and provisions for their welfare and advancement—your birthday celebration for each and every employee—these are some of the factors that have developed such a remarkable *esprit de corps* and the universal desire of your employees to serve you diligently and well."

FAMILY

Because much of her life was spent in the store, it is a source of the larger portion of material written about Beatrice. But she was far more than the hardworking manager of a city emporium. She was the mother of two daughters—Georgette, whom she called Georgie, and Dorothy, whom she called Dots—and the grandmother of twelve.

The childhood years of the Auerbach daughters were, by all accounts, happy ones. They spent carefree summers at Auerfarm; traveled with their parents; enjoyed outings with their grandfather, Moses Fox; and were well supervised by Ms. Tasker, their governess.

Both Georgette and Dorothy attended the Oxford School, a private school for girls, which was in their neighborhood, though Georgette started at the Noah Webster School in Hartford. As a West Hartford resident, her father was required to pay for that privilege. She transferred to Oxford for two reasons. One day Georgette did not come home for lunch, so Beatrice went to school to look for her and found her in the basement of the school playing marbles with the boys. In addition, Beatrice attended a class at Noah Webster and thought that the boys and girls had their hands in the air far too much with requests to go to the bathroom. Dorothy had started Oxford early because she was an October baby, but also because she kept walking over to the school on her own. Since Georgette was born in May, though they were four years apart, there were only three years between them in school.

While Georgette did graduate from the Oxford School, a letter from the principal of Walnut Hill School in Natick, Massachusetts, indicated that Beatrice had considered sending her eldest daughter there. Beatrice was told, "The trustees of our school, years ago, decided to reserve a certain number of places for students of Jewish family. At present these places are all filled." The principal offered to put Georgette's name on the waiting list, and her letter concluded by asking whether Beatrice knew Margery Hartman, a senior at Walnut Hill. Most probably, the fact that Margery Hartman, her closest friend's daughter, attended the school had prompted Beatrice's interest. The letter made clear that minority quotas were in place, and the principal appeared to take pride in the equanimity of allowing a "certain number" of Jewish girls to attend.

Correspondence preserved from this time gives a sense of each daughter's personality. In a letter dated August 14, 1930, to Beatrice from Carrie Uhlfelder in Salt Lake City, there was enthusiastic approval of Dorothy who, at age eleven, was visiting family there. Carrie described her as "so capable, so willing, so eager, so thorough, so happy in all she does." She told Beatrice, "You can well say, 'She is my Dorothy in whom I am well pleased.' She shows the character and charm that George and you both express."

Growing up, the sisters were always close, though, as sisters do, they had their share of quarrels. In an interview, Georgette recalled that she threw something out of the window of the

Highland Street house because she was angry with Dorothy and with her parents, feeling she was blamed for everything being the older sibling. Perhaps this was the iron horse doorstop that Dorothy said Georgette threw at her once.

When Georgette was sixteen or seventeen, one of her wishes was to have a horse of her own. Beatrice took this opportunity to allow her daughter to learn about just how costly maintaining an animal could be. In fact, at the end of a summer at camp, Georgette was required to make arrangements to ship her mare Puss 'n Boots home. Her letter, dated August 28, 1933, revealed her thoroughness in preparing for all likelihoods.

She began by letting her mother know how thrilled she was about Puss 'n Boots. "Gee, it was swell of you to let me use my own judgment 'cause really I know it was very wise." She went on to tell her mother about her careful negotiations on price and on arrangements for delivery of the horse from Maine to Hartford. She explained that she and the seller were both signing "a typed agreement that he is to receive a check of $850.00 for the safe delivery of Puss to Hartford." She enclosed a copy of a letter she had written to F. B. Anniger in

Hartford, asking him to arrange to receive the mare and provide a box stall for her. Georgette showed her business acumen when she explained, "Since my family has ridden and done business with you for over thirteen years, I naturally feel that my horse would be safest under your supervision." She seemed to have thought of everything, even to the delay in insuring the horse while in transit because only death was covered by the insurance available in Maine. The thoroughness exemplified by this episode would characterize most of Georgette's dealings in the future.

In another letter written to her mother from Vassar in 1939, two weeks before her graduation, Georgette explored her options for the future. She had been accepted by Macy's on their executive training squad, and she interviewed for a similar position at Lord & Taylor. She was inclined to Lord & Taylor because "it's more the caliber store I'd like to work for, and I'd have the opportunity to do a variety of things."

Georgette was blunt about refusing a chance to work with Tobe Coburn as a stylist, which Georgette described as "learning a racket." She was firm, too, about not returning to Hartford to work at G. Fox anytime soon. Then she said, "There's no sense in mincing words or kidding ourselves; you and I could simply never live together happily no matter how much we both tried." She reminded Beatrice that it wasn't the big things but the small ones on which they constantly disagreed, and she envisioned their life together as "one long, perpetual squabble." Intellectually, she said, they got along splendidly, but emotionally they were poles apart.

She softened the blow by saying that if she was in New York City, she could easily come home for weekends, and she did not close the door on Hartford forever, "just for the next couple of years."

Dorothy left Oxford for Bryn Mawr, Pennsylvania, where she attended the Baldwin School and then Bryn Mawr College. While she was a student at Bryn Mawr, she became the first female ever to take classes at nearby Haverford, a men's college. When the dean told her she would not receive any credit for her work at Haverford, Dorothy took her case to the college president. After protracted discussion, she received half credit—a significant breakthrough which doubtless helped speed the day when cross registration among local colleges and universities became commonplace. While in Philadelphia, Dorothy met Bernard Schiro whom she married in 1940. After their marriage, they remained in Philadelphia for a few years.

Georgette married Richard Koopman in 1940. Dick Koopman was an enthusiastic angler, and Georgette soon developed an interest in the sport. Georgette was "a formidable fisherwoman" recalled her friend and neighbor Hinda Fischer. "She took every opportunity to go salmon fishing even when she was in the final days of her life." She added that Georgette was usually the only female allowed to go with the men because they so respected her ability.

For her part, Dorothy made several forays with Bernie and the children, in a Winnebago style camper, of which Dorothy was the usual driver. Dorothy referred to the vehicle as "my mink coat." On one excursion, the Schiros traveled twelve thousand miles from West Hartford to Vancouver Island and back.

In 1944, Georgette and Dick moved to Texas where Dick served in the Army Air Corps (precursor of the air force) and where the couple awaited the birth of their first child. Dorothy wrote to her sister detailing what she was doing to accommodate Georgette's many requests for things unavailable or scarce in Texas. She began by saying she was worn out trying to buy long-since-forgotten items, being tactful about why this or that "won't do." She explained her efforts to provide Georgette with what she could. Among items she was concerned with were Yardley soap and powder, an electric diaper washer, two pails, a bed jacket, bras, pillowcases, diaper shirts, Birdseye soakers, washcloths, and a special suitcase. The suitcase, she explained, was "the one that used to fit the rear deck of Mother's old Cad.—the one burner job, better known as the love of the Pratt and Whitney man who bought it from Taber's—the sucker!"

Dorothy proceeded to offer a minilecture to her sister on how to receive gifts sent to her for the baby. "If Mother later on sends you cute things for the baby, say thank you nicely and be grateful. Don't write a long letter about how you don't need it, etc. Be more like your little sister!!!! It keeps everyone happy, and it doesn't hurt you."

Both of the Auerbach daughters were involved in their mother's life, increasingly as they grew older. More and more frequently, Beatrice's daughters served as hostesses at functions related to the store or to the Women's Service Bureau. Like her mother, Georgette was a "take charge" sort. She was very intelligent and intuitive. "On occasion Georgette could be abrasive, but she didn't seem to realize it," said Hinda Fischer. Dorothy was likeable but more self-effacing. Those who knew the family well said that Dorothy was more like her father and Georgette more like her mother. Georgette had a great sense of style while Dorothy was less concerned about fashion. In fact, Beatrice was said to have wished aloud that both girls were more interested in clothing as she herself was always a fashion plate.

Left to right: Dorothy, Beatrice, Georgette

At the store, Beatrice almost always wore black, and most of her employees were required to wear either black or dark blue and white. On other public occasions, she strove for an impression that suited her position as head of a large department store, naturally wearing the latest tasteful fashions.

As busy as she was, nothing interfered with family time. Every Sunday, without fail, Beatrice had lunch with her grandchildren and dinner in the evening with their parents. The grandchildren have special memories of these visits.

Linda Schiro Glickstein recalled, "We went after Sunday school and arrived as Grannie was getting dressed. The boys stayed downstairs and played games, but the girls went up to her dressing room and sat with her as she got ready. Before lunch, we always had shrimp cocktail in the sunroom. We each had three shrimps. For lunch, she always had scrambled eggs, crisp bacon, and, in season, fresh asparagus which she ate with her fingers. We had a regular hot lunch. Dessert was always vanilla ice cream with chocolate shots (jimmies), colored sprinkles, and hot fudge. Some of us made what we called Sherlock Holmes, when we stirred the ice cream, hot fudge, and sprinkles to a mixture before we ate it.

"It was at my grandmother's house that I learned about finger bowls. They always came after the main course with a doily underneath. But during the summer at the farm, there was a large leaf underneath, rather than the doily."

Another granddaughter, Rena Koopman, noted that Sunday lunches were full of training possibilities, from the proper use of finger bowls to how to deal with people who worked for you. "When we left the table at the end of lunch, we went immediately into the kitchen and spoke to each person there . . . thanking Carl for cooking, and Martha and Annie for serving us."

Brooksie Koopman recalled that they also learned how to take food from the left when formally served, use a water glass sparingly ("Don't fill up on water; please drink your milk.") and hold a conversation with one person speaking at a time. Lunch was served on china with crystal, silver, and linen. She remembered, too, learning to fold her napkin at the end of a meal.

Rena also recalled, "Grannie had a silver piggy bank which she kept on the sunporch where we gathered on Sundays before lunch, and she had a small box with new coins in it which she kept nearby. Once we were old enough to earn money for chores or have allowances, we joined in the piggy bank routine. We were encouraged to bring whatever part of our allowance we felt comfortable parting with, and Grannie offered matching funds. One of our nickels, and one of her new shiny nickels (or as we got older, dimes, quarters, etc.) went into the piggy bank. At the end of the year, we would open the bank, count the money, and then vote on where to send the funds. It was Grannie's way to offer us an early lesson in philanthropy."

Other highlights were the celebrations of Christmas and Passover with an elegant dinner at 1040 Prospect Avenue. One Passover, each grandchild was given an engraved Passover cup; and when they were older, she gave them a larger cup. Christmas was always a very special occasion where everyone, friends and family, gathered and exchanged gifts and enjoyed wonderful treats.

Linda Schiro Glickstein recalled, "On each of our birthdays, Grannie came to our house for dinner. My father always carved the meat. When it was roast beef or steak, I remember spooning blood gravy into a little shot glass for her to drink. I also liked the blood gravy."

Her grandchildren all remembered that Beatrice always had time for them, and that she was always very interested in what they were doing. She didn't talk about her achievements or awards, but she sought to encourage them in their own endeavors.

When they were older, their grandmother helped them make major decisions in their lives. Linda Glickstein recalled shopping for her first car, which was a gift from her grandmother. With the help of her uncle, she chose an English car, a Rover, because it was deemed the safest vehicle she could purchase.

Like all of us, Beatrice had her likes and dislikes, some more idiosyncratic than others. She did not condone profanity. Ella Feldman, the daughter of Rabbi Feldman, worked at G. Fox one summer while in high school. At the time, Ella spent idle moments composing poetry, and one of her verses was brought to the attention of Mrs. Auerbach who phoned Ella and said, "I'd like to have this published locally—if you'll take out some of the 'goddamns.'" Ella refused, and the poem never saw the light of day.[1]

Beatrice had two dogs: Beige, a cocker, and Beauty, a pug. Rena Koopman remembered that Beatrice let Beauty sit on furniture she wouldn't allow her grandchildren to occupy. Beige, on the other hand, was never allowed in the house when the grandchildren were there as he disliked youngsters. "The dogs were spoiled and not good-tempered, but Grannie loved them. They could do no wrong as far as she was concerned."

Massages were a must for Beatrice, usually on Sunday. She used a professional masseuse and had a room designated specifically for that purpose.

Although she wore black regularly in the store, she wore colors on other occasions and had a great deal of pink in her décor. Noticing that her grandmother always carried very neat bills in her wallet, Rena Koopman asked her how she managed to keep them that way. She responded that every day Annie Bartels, her housekeeper, insisted on ironing the money for her. To Annie, there were no exceptions to neatness.

Rena observed that her grandmother had pockets in all of her clothing. Knowing that only some of her own clothes had pockets, she asked her grandmother about it. Beatrice explained that she had missed many days of school when she was on trips with her parents. She had been out of school when her class learned the multiplication tables, and she sometimes had trouble calculating. In her position, it wouldn't look good to see her counting on her fingers. So if a garment came without pockets, they were always added. The pockets enabled her to keep her secret. By contrast, her big picture math skills were remarkable. Rena recalls being told by one of Beatrice's executives that Beatrice could look at a huge page of figures and evaluate it quickly and accurately.

Beatrice collected stamps, particularly those from the many countries she visited. Often, these were cancelled stamps obtained from her letters to the family from abroad. She also had a sizeable group of postcards. She had collections of decorative plates, antique porcelain figurines, and ceramic cows to which sometimes new additions were made by her children and grandchildren. One can imagine how helpful this was when choosing a gift for someone who could be said to have everything.

Dark chocolate and licorice were favorites; her drink of choice was scotch and, of course, a Manhattan. When traveling abroad, she often enjoyed a gin and tonic, especially in the warmest climates. She smoked as did most of her contemporaries, and she preferred Murads, a brand of Turkish cigarettes which produced a pungent odor barely tolerable to some, including her secretary, Shirley Koplowitz.

In spite of her status, Beatrice often drove her own car. "She was," said Hinda Fischer, "the worst driver ever." On one occasion, she was involved in a bad accident at the intersection of Prospect and Asylum avenues, but that experience did not deter her from getting behind the wheel rather than be chauffeured to a destination. She continued to drive until she was in her late seventies.

Another of her predilections is revealed in an anecdote from family friend Henry Scherer. When he was a youngster, Beatrice was a frequent dinner guest of his parents. As soon as dinner was over, Henry asked to be excused in order to go to his room and listen to the radio broadcast of his beloved Brooklyn Dodgers. Soon after, there was a knock on his door and in came Beatrice to enjoy the game, being a devoted fan of the Dodgers herself.

Beatrice enjoyed the seaside and made a number of summer trips to Nantucket. She took with her Anna Gianetti, a hairdresser from the G. Fox salon. They always checked in at the White Elephant.

She hated waste, whether of time, goods, or
money. Trudi Lovell, who brought Mrs. Auerbach
the reports on each day's receipts, recalls one
particular visit. When Trudi entered, Beatrice took
note of the fact that she had very small feet, like
herself. She asked Trudi what shoe size she wore,
and when she responded size 4, Beatrice told her
she would bring her some of her own footwear
which she no longer needed. At another time,
when Brooksie was asking her grandmother about
her wedding, she inquired as to whether Beatrice
still had her wedding dress, knowing that it was
a common practice for women to preserve their
dresses to hand down to the next generation.
Beatrice replied that right after the wedding, she
had had her dress cut down so that she could wear
it on other occasions.

She loved books and bemoaned the fact that
she didn't have time to read as much as she
would have liked. Margery Oakes remembered
how much Beatrice enjoyed going to the *Herald
Tribune*-sponsored gatherings where new books
were reviewed and discussed, and she took every
opportunity to attend, always making certain to
keep up with what was being written. She did read

the newspapers faithfully, but she always wore gloves when doing so, so that her hands wouldn't be stained by the ink. Her friend Estelle Hartman even gifted her with a pair of gloves printed like a newspaper.

Although Beatrice had early abandoned her first name, Hannah, in favor of her middle name, Beatrice, a few official documents, such as her marriage certificate, retain Hannah as her first name. Of course, she gained a variety of names as her life went on, some of which she liked, others she found annoying. Her cousins called her Beats or Bits, and George called her Trix or Trixie; her children addressed her as Mother, and their friends called her Aunt Bea. To her grandchildren, she was Grannie. Leaders in the retail field called her BFA, and her employees and many who knew her professionally called her Mrs. A, but never to her face as she was known to dislike the epithet.

Considering her position in the world of business and in the community, she was modest and self-effacing. She did not like pretension. On one occasion, when Madame Chiang Kai-shek, wife of the generalissimo of the Republic of China, came to the United States seeking financial assistance for her country, she wore a full-length mink coat. Beatrice drew her aside and said, "You know, dear, one doesn't beg for money wearing a mink coat."

In a 1986 letter to the editor of the *Hartford Courant*, a story is told about a visit to the University of Hartford, an institution which she did much to endow. Her chauffeured limousine was parked in a restricted zone. Not recognizing the ownership of the vehicle, a campus security guard wrote a ticket. On return to the car, Beatrice saw the citation and directed her chauffeur to take her to the security headquarters. "She herself got out of the limousine, marched inside, and personally paid the importunate tab."[2] Anyone else in her position would have torn up the ticket or passed it on to the university president to handle.

Rena Koopman remembered that a frequent visitor to her grannie's home was a pleasant older woman whom they called Mrs. R. She read to them and listened to their chatter. When one day Rena saw a picture of her identifying her as the widow of the U.S. president, she asked her mother why they had not been told who she was. "Would that have made a difference?" Georgette asked.

Beatrice did treasure her privacy. In 1952, she had a radical mastectomy. Reticence on her part or more likely respect for her privacy kept this information from the public.

In her later years, she became a patient of Dr. Arnold Fieldman, whose practice was fairly new. She was somewhat apprehensive about him because of his youth. But he recalled her saying, "Well, young man, we'll give this a try and see how it works out." She remained under his care until her death of congestive heart failure.

The Schiro Family   Grannie   The Koopman Family
1967

FRIENDS

Certainly, Beatrice could count a large number of people as acquaintances and friends. But as with most people, she had a few very close friends with whom she shared her thoughts and experiences. Her closest friend was Estelle Hartman, a neighbor and confidant who knew all of the intimate details of Beatrice's life. Estelle's husband, Manny, and his family had been friends of the Fox family for years; and as soon as he brought his bride home to Hartford, she and Beatrice became close companions. Once Manny began his business, the Hartman Tobacco Company, he had frequent occasions to interact with Moses Fox and the Auerbachs at gatherings related to the business community to which they belonged. The two women shared many experiences, and Estelle was a great support to Beatrice when George died.

In earlier years in Connecticut, holiday celebrations alternated between the Auerbach home at 1040 Prospect Avenue and the Hartman residence at 160 Oxford Street. The gatherings, which included family and friends, grew over the years as children married and grandchildren arrived. Margery Hartman Oakes, Estelle's daughter, thought of Beatrice as a member of her own family and called her Aunt Bea. She went to camp with the Auerbach daughters, Georgette and Dorothy, when they were children. Margery also shared Georgette's love of horseback riding.

Beatrice took a part in a number of events in the lives of the Hartman family. When a sister-in-law passed away, Beatrice went with Estelle to oversee burial arrangements. When Margery and her husband John were looking for an apartment in New York, Beatrice helped them to find the perfect one, on Fifth Avenue, overlooking the lake in Central Park.

On many of Beatrice's trips to New York, she took Estelle along and later spent time with Margery. Margery has fond memories of the many times she accompanied Beatrice to the opera.

Estelle and Beatrice were generous with their time and money. Like Beatrice, Estelle was a member of the Fifteen Club and was active in the work of United Jewish Charities. In fact, when Estelle died at the age of ninety-six, she was celebrated for her philanthropic deeds in much the same fashion as her close friend Beatrice was.

A second important friend was Chase Going Woodhouse. A professor of economics at Connecticut College for Women from 1934-1946, Chase was an activist on behalf of women. She served as the first female secretary of state in Connecticut in 1941 and 1942, and she served twice in the House of Representatives from 1945-1947 and 1949-1951. Between the two terms, Mrs. Woodhouse was executive director of the Women's Division of the Democratic National Committee. Always a champion of women, when asked what she would want inscribed on her tombstone, she immediately replied, "She was born a woman. She died a person."[1]

As women in the public eye, and even more as persons devoted to the advancement of women, Beatrice and Chase became friends in the early 1940s. So thoroughly did Beatrice trust

Chase that she gave her an active role in the formation and operation of the Service Bureau for Women's Organizations. Also, in her position on the Connecticut College Faculty, Chase was a logical choice to oversee the Auerbach Program in Retailing, the internship offered to deserving students aspiring to a career in that field. The Service Bureau brought the two women closer together, and the friendship lasted a lifetime.

From 1946 to 1957, Beatrice and Chase embarked on a series of trips to all corners of the globe. Both women were in their late fifties. Chase was distinguished by her lovely white hair. She had a round, pleasant face and wore glasses. While Beatrice just reached five feet, Chase was at least five inches taller. Beatrice described their trips in her travel journals. In the journals, Beatrice made few directly political observations, preferring to describe and retell experiences. But on her 1949 visit to UNESCO in Turkey, she discussed the exchange of scholars. "I believe that a great deal can be done for democracy through indoctrination. I further believe that it is necessary to send more adults with more comprehension of our language, a greater sense of responsibility to make further use of their knowledge and information when they return to the Turks at home. But the same story exists in almost every direction—that it is a very young country and there is so very much to do that they are not sufficiently organized in actuality, but are over-organized on paper."

Beatrice & Chase

In 1953, visiting Liberia, she witnessed the hardships of the village people. "I feel that the French are not helping the natives to help themselves, but are buying them; and in the end, this never pays as natives, in turn, will learn the way to blackmail."

In Cairo, she observed the great hatred of Egyptians for the British and believed that the breech between them would "not be healed without bloodshed." She wondered why Egypt shouldn't govern herself without an outside army. "Civilization has been here with education and culture long before Greece, Rome, much less Europe and the New World, and in great measure, I sympathize with their emotional indignity at being denied all the responsibilities and privileges that go with a free and sovereign state."

Arriving home from her trip to Europe, Beatrice made her customary address from the mezzanine to employees gathered on the main floor, letting them in on her experiences and sharing her impressions with them. *Hartford Times* reporter William H. Ryan was on hand and, in 1956, recorded a number of her opinions about Russia:

"Russia, today, incorporates a planned way of living—a great big machine with the ability to be mobile. Its potentiality is tremendous. The people can do anything their government determines it wants to do. The people themselves live a regimented life in the sense that someone else makes the decisions as to what kind of life they can live. They can buy articles in stores; they can go to the ballet or theater. They have things, but someone else decides what things they will have." She continued, "It's just like the Army. There is always somebody higher up. It's a different ideology, a different philosophy of life. All I know is I hope I never have to live under it."

Always concerned with the women in the places she visited, she noted that, in Russia, women and men were considered equal. She saw women doctors, engineers, and surveyors working on the roads. "Chivalry is not unknown; it is just not considered. Why get up to give a woman a seat in the subway? She's an equal. She should be willing and able to stand."

At the same time, she pointed out that nurseries for children were located near factories, and young mothers were "permitted and encouraged" to take periodic breaks from work to nurse their babies. Beatrice had great praise, too, for the Russian children and for the education system: "Education is remarkable. Everyone goes to school at least ten years. Professors are very highly regarded and also highly paid. Students are highly regarded and also paid if they are good enough."

While she admired the ballet, opera, and theater, she bemoaned the fact that the Russians drank too much. "There is plenty of vodka around," she remarked.

Observing that the Russian economy was still geared for heavy goods, she added, "They have the facility and capacity to change factories to make consumer goods."[2]

At a briefing session before leaving for Russia, Beatrice and Chase were told that, as the Russians were very impressed by academic degrees, it was important when signing the hotel register to add your degrees after your signature. Better treatment was sure to follow. Beatrice pondered this, entirely cognizant that she had no degrees to list. Chase, however, had several. Beatrice decided she would let Chase register first and then imitate her. So Mrs. Woodhouse signed the register, adding after her name her undergraduate degree and her several graduate degrees. Beatrice signed next, added some of the same degrees for herself, and then without thinking she tacked on for good measure *Etc.* The Russians knew about BAs, MBAs, and LLDs, but they had never encountered an *Etc.* They were tremendously impressed, and since they felt that they ought to know what an *Etc.* was, fortunately for Beatrice, they never asked.

As might be expected, Beatrice had great interest in the huge GUM Department Store in Moscow, which she estimated to be ten times the size of G. Fox but "not up-to-date at all." She described the shoe department as setup "like a notions counter. The shoes were piled on. The customer was expected to know his size. If he or she didn't, that was too bad. They went away with ill-fitting shoes."

In the GUM department that sold televisions, she saw customers waiting in long lines to make a purchase. She explained, "You had to order a set and then come to pick it up yourself: no home delivery. There is also no such thing as a charge account."

She recognized a "pioneer spirit in Russia similar to our Westward Movement," only in Russia the movement was eastward to Siberia where "the government offers virgin land waiting to be settled by prospective pioneers."[3]

Industry and commerce drew her attention wherever she traveled. In August of 1949, traveling in Greece, Beatrice discovered a most unusual industry. "The small pieces of fur thrown away in New York's Eighth Avenue fur workrooms are swept up from the floor into bundles and sent back to Greece. Here they are sewed together very carefully, each piece only about the size of a thumbnail, until they are large fur blankets from either Persian lamb, mink tails, or any other precious furs, then reshipped back to New York to be made into coats." She found this procedure most instructive and said, "From now on, I'm going to see that I get real skins and not thousands of little skin pieces sewed together when buying a coat."

She proclaimed the Teheran bazaars to be "absolutely wonderful." And she was especially taken by the copper bazaars which "made me wish for a magic carpet to transport everything I saw home."

On June 10, 1953, she attended the tobacco auction in Salisbury, Rhodesia, the largest such auction in the world. She described the process: "The tobacco is sold bale by bale, and the men who do the selling spend six months in Virginia and six months over here. The auction rooms are run on a cooperative basis, and one building covers one acre and another building two acres. They sell the tobacco in specified pounds to a bale and the starter of the auction is nearly as important as the auctioneer. It takes six months of daily selling to dispose of the crop. But how they decide who bids and how much to me is a Chinese puzzle because I can't understand a word; nevertheless, it is done and that is the important thing."

In May of 1953, she wrote from Leopoldville about a visit to a cotton mill "where the cotton is grown up in the interior and brought down on barges, spun and printed right there. The designs are fantastic and very colorful. Where we Westerners don't want everyone going around with our same cut of dress, so they want a design that is individual. The result is you see thousands of the natives each with a different design in multicolor. The equipment is most modern and would put our own New England textile mills to shame. The labor is all African except for the few foremen." By contrast, she found Addis Ababa strange because everyone wore white garments, so the market was singularly free of color.

Beatrice left Chase behind while in Stuttgart in order to visit the Basch factory, which had been bombed but was, in 1949, working full blast "and with the latest and most approved machinery, bought for the most part in Switzerland. They do their work on assembly lines and pay by the piece." She marveled at the dexterity of the workers. As an employer herself, she was interested in the fraternal attitude of management toward the workers. "They have a housing plan, also a pension one, but the latter is not anywhere near as generous as is our own." They also supplied lunch for their workers at the very moderate price of fifty pfennig.

On her visit to Israel, she was amazed by the unbounded aggressiveness and boundless determination of the Israelis to succeed in building their new country. Her one criticism of Israel was that "the acquirement of the social conventions and the niceties of life would not make them less sincere." She recognized the importance of their establishing a common language when the populace came from all parts of the world. "Everyone is speaking and talking in Hebrew with not even one syllable that is familiar to the ear. The signs on shops, the hotel menus—everything Hebrew; and to me it becomes understandable, as, if you are developing a melting pot and really want people to understand and associate with one another and not grow up in groups that are unamalgamated, there must be one language."

In her diary, Beatrice acknowledged that it would be difficult to visit Africa without encountering proof of the influence of missionaries. Many denominations had established themselves in Africa. She admitted that, "Although they have done much good, [they] leave the simple mind of the African confused, and I believe the veneer of Christianity is only skin-deep and not great enough to carry (the natives) on into and through the struggle which, without question, lies ahead. Plural wives and witchcraft are ingrained after many centuries of existence." In South Africa, she was moved by the singing of a boys' choir at a mission school. She also commented on what makes a missionary: "It takes a certain type human, one who is willing to sacrifice, is satisfied with very little of the material in nature and has faith a just reward will be given when life is ended . . . . I guess I am too worldly to understand their thinking."

Of Ethiopia, her judgment was terse: "Ethiopia is still medieval, in spite of the airplanes that swoop down at the airport. The life for them and many others could be so much more simple and pleasant with a bit of executive organizing and with some more plumbing and sanitary conditions."

It was impossible to avoid the effects of apartheid in South Africa. "Life under apartheid," she said, "reminds me of people coming here in the seventeenth century, clutching a Bible, going to sleep like Rip Van Winkle, and waking up centuries later not realizing that an industrial revolution has taken place, that slavery in the world has been abolished, that minorities are protected." She detested Johannesberg. "The mines and their dumps are in the middle of it . . . . Everything is commercial, and I might apply the word 'vulgar.' It eats and lives money." Gold and uranium were the sources of wealth, "but somehow or other the feeling of slave labor hits you harder than anywhere else . . ." Capetown, by contrast, thrilled her. "It is glorious, like Rio and San Francisco, nestled at the sea's edge with sheer rocks rising sharply behind . . . to see the thousands of lights come on and the moon rise with its reflection on the water is a sight not easily forgotten." She found the atmosphere charming and declared, "I have lost my heart to the Mt. Nelson Hotel with its great, spacious rooms and lovely décor."

At the beginning of her trip to the Far East in 1951, she arrived in Lebanon and became dismayed by the attitudes of the men in customs. She said, "They seem to have one thought in common . . . to make each passenger carrying a U.S. passport clear as rapidly as possible and convey to them their dislike and suspicion of the motives of the individual and our government in general." She concluded that the favored position of Israel with the United States was at the root of this attitude, and she thought that the situation had worsened in a few years since her last visit; "it is like a powder keg." She encountered a similar attitude in 1953 when she visited Khartoum, which she described as dirty, hot, and insect infested. "The Asians as well as the Arabs are the big bosses," she remarked, "the result being that white skins and pink complexions are not greeted with respect or consideration, but with scorn and great indifference, no one taking much trouble to hide their distrust and dislike." The situation was exacerbated by the fact that

Beatrice and Chase's arrival was unscheduled, and while they were often met by U.S. ambassadors or members of the ambassador's staff, here they were on their own.

At tea with a professor of religious research in Jerusalem, Beatrice encountered a Russian girl who "was vitriolic in her denunciation of Jewry, and we heard the doctrines of hate pour out. It made me shiver involuntarily." Unable to sleep that night, Beatrice thought about "humans hating humans all in the name of religion . . . I do not understand it and finally had to admit to myself that I could not fathom it."

Everyone who knew Beatrice admired her impeccable grooming and elegant clothing. But given the conditions operating in some of their lodgings, and in the climate, she often was faced with a need to compromise and sometimes to "endure." Beatrice told an anecdote about such an adjustment. A truck ride was arranged for her in Germany. Then she stated, "Slacks were necessary on the lift to Berlin and a nice lieutenant drove home for a pair of hers for me. She is all of five feet ten in height, so you can get a chuckle just thinking of me wearing hers, but they, the army, prohibit any passenger riding in the bucket seats unless you do as you are told. On the same trip, Beatrice decided to go to Berlin "without extra luggage or clothes other than the necessities and the clothes I wore."

Greek hospitality presented a challenge to the two women. When they were brought a goblet of water and a small dish of sweetmeats, Beatrice realized that she should eat it. "But, she wrote, 'Chase and I just could not, so we very carefully waited until no one was looking, wrapped the sweetmeats in a piece of paper and later on that night disposed of them in the road where no one could see.'"

In Turkey, the two travelers carried on a conversation through an interpreter who spoke French. Beatrice said there came a time when both women needed to use the water closet, and here Chase received her first shock. "This time the advantage of my early training and travels had prepared me for the Turkish W.C., which is nothing but a hole—no seat but just a hole to stand over." Beatrice reported that they had many laughs over their necessary adjustments.

Sometimes she struggled with the customs of an area. She told of an unusual tea at the home of the physician Dr. Ampofo in Accra, Ghana. "Can you imagine," she wrote, "trying to balance and keep an ear of corn in one hand and a teacup in the other? Corn was served by them as biscuits would be by us. I have an idea that it was a special treat in our honor, but certainly one which caused both Chase and me embarrassment."

In the Belgian Congo, Beatrice and Chase were taken to the Hotel Regina in Leopoldville. She remarked that no one had quite prepared her for what she found. "It isn't that the hotel is so old, but it is so disreputable. Everything is half finished, and there seems to be no likelihood of it ever being completed. The pressure of the cold water is such that in the morning, when you are ready to wash, there is no water coming from the tap; and of course, there is none to flush the toilet, and the odors ensuing are beyond imagination and really unfit for me to describe." She did find, though, that the beds were clean; and here, as elsewhere, she made ample use of the insecticide spray she carried with her from America.[4]

Arriving at the swanky Hotel Victoria in Bulawayo, Rhodesia, they were surprised but pleased at the luxury. Still significant adaptations were needed. "Chase and I had double rooms with built-in electric heaters, for which we were grateful because while the sun shines in the day, the evenings, nights, and early mornings are cold. I adopted wearing a sweater under my dress, putting on a coat and scarf and then, only by constantly imbibing brandy and soda did I manage to keep comfortably warm."

In Pakistan, they faced a minor dilemma because of the absence of hangers or even hooks, explained by the fact that the local women wore saris, which they folded. In addition, there was no sitting room; and a personal friend, Begum Mustafq, appealed to the management for better quarters for her American friends, unbeknownst to Beatrice who was just about to get into the bathtub when several staff members "swooped down upon me and took all my clothes and my luggage." She wrote to her family, "You should have seen me shuffling out the door and down the corridor. I'm sure you would have had me committed to Norwich as I was clothed only in two bath towels wrapped around my torso." Fortunately, the new rooms were significantly better.

Two issues of constant concern for the women were heat and insects. Beatrice said, "In my grip, there was always insecticide bomb spray which I used lavishly, and I never regretted the cost.

[Payment had to be made for any luggage over the weight limit.] She kept a dressing gown handy, too, because "with temperatures at around ninety-five degrees, one dispenses with nightgowns." The heat also made applying makeup impossible because the temperature even at 8:00 AM was over one hundred degrees, and she noted, "We literally dripped."

No inconvenience, however, compared with the theft of her luggage in Italy on their way home from their African trip. Beatrice called it a "minor tragedy" because of what was taken. "All the new swank clothes were packed in that particular bag—the gray Rosenstein evening dress which I hadn't even worn, the lovely Jane Derby dresses, my Carnegie suit, the lovely Paris (black and white) sport coat, all disappeared. Also the cashmere scarf Tobe brought to the steamer for me, three pairs of Evins' shoes, and this is only a partial list . . ."

Occasional misunderstandings occurred on which Beatrice commented. They got some interesting insights into the thinking of the Pakistanis when she and Chase were invited to listen to a talk by Begum Irkamullah about a trip she had taken to the United States. In the question-and-answer session following, it became clear that "our magazine articles have given the impression that sex frustration is one of the vital questions we in the U.S. have to solve. Questions on this subject occupied most of the time." Irritated, Chase and Beatrice slipped out and returned to their hotel.

At a meeting of a women's club in Pakistan, the discussion turned to issues of color and minority races in America. Beatrice characterized this as "a burning question and one that the Communists have embellished and fed to all of the Southern Asian people. It is a subject which, as you know, has always not alone concerned, but interested me. I decided to answer it frankly and to tell some of the things I had been doing at home and what my hopes were for the future, admitting conditions but also explaining that this was something that had been left to us as a problem for several generations, but how each year showed greater progress toward a solution of the problem. I am immodest enough to feel that I do a good job, and they kept me talking so long and were so attentive that our noon appointment had to be missed. However, as Chase and I both consider ourselves ambassadors of good will in a small way, we feel it was time well spent and have no regrets."

Beatrice & Chase with Begum Irkmullah

At a dinner party given for them by the chief justice of police in Lahore, she discovered that several guests believed we have "no respect for the law and that lynching is an everyday practice." She countered by relating stories she had heard about Moslems who cut off their wives' noses and ears in jealous rages. She asked if these were customary acts or just irrational aberrations. Her point was, of course, that no country should be judged by extreme instances. Yet she followed with the observation to her family that she "has it on good authority that plastic surgery has had a great boom over here."

Beatrice had strong political views when it came to the role of Americans abroad. While she praised the men serving as ambassadors, she recognized a need that was unattended: "If I were asked, I would suggest that more preparation be given to the young wives and the obligations they assume in representing us . . . . Today no wife just belongs to her husband, or can be only mother to her children, but she is being observed and emulated by the same people who appraise her husband. Her part in establishing 'good propaganda' needs more thought by the high-ups in the State Department. I have many details in mind and would like to talk more about it if I could get someone to consider this seriously and really listen."

A similar attitude was embodied in her criticism of CARE in Bangalore. "The CARE packages and sets of tools—a gift of $1,000.00 worth of things sent by an unnamed donor from the United States" were readied for distribution to the villagers. They were "poor and not sufficiently nourished. The children had rickets. It was the usual Indian scene of famine, but they sat in rows and not demanding to receive their share of the bounty, but patiently waiting for the time of distribution. We watched the villagers go back to their own villages after receiving their gifts, but I cannot help but feel that CARE should study the customs and habits of the country to which they send their packages, as white rice was sent here, which they do not like nor use, also white sugar was sent and their need is for brown. Neither were the tools correct. A far better job could be done if the people who are living among them were consulted before items were sent."

In fact, on a later trip in 1959, Beatrice and Chase coordinated with CARE to provide supplies and two sewing machines for the children's orphanage in La Paz, Bolivia.

**Beatrice meets with the Mother Superior
of The Children's Orphanage in La Paz, Bolivia**

When touring Kashmir, a troubled area, Beatrice worried aloud about the contrast between the astounding beauty of the area and her dismay at the condition of the residents, many of whom were "without everything." She particularly worries about how these people could survive the winter without heat, proper housing, or food. Of her shopping there, she remarked, it "was not good business. I know that I permitted myself to be taken in, that I could have bargained, but honestly human beings seem to have the least value of anything over here, and I may be called a capitalist; however, there is still within me that feeling of 'live and let live', and if I were not to have given in to my impulses, those words would be empty words indeed."

In Turkey, too, they passed through a village about twenty miles outside of Istanbul where they saw a circumcision ceremony being conducted "right in the open. The filth, the primitive bandages, the lack of anything modern" belied its proximity to a city of over one million.

In Ankara, they visited a village where farming was key. When the residents heard that Beatrice had a farm, they were intrigued, but she said, "When I told them what production we have from a flock of 160 chickens and the average of butter fat which comes from our cows, they were astounded." She explained to them the county agricultural agency and the USDA, and they responded that they have run their own farms for centuries, and "they do not want anyone else telling them what to do."

At the conclusion of her trip to the Far East, Beatrice said that the journey had not been carefree or casual, "but one that has aroused our minds and thinking, one that has been rich in experience and afforded the opportunity of meeting individuals; the politicians; the educators; the leaders of meager labor parties; the women, both those who take their part in the world seriously and those who we call ornamental; business men; the emissaries of our State Department, who know a great deal and who each day are adding to their knowledge—each and all important—and in concluding, my last word, as we come to the end of the little book, is an expression of praise and respect for the little people of the world."

As with all good diaries, hers were organized on a time line, recounting fairly meticulously each day's events, people, and places. Many of their encounters were planned social occasions, and they took the opportunity to experience the cuisine, music, and cultural events offered.

Catching the spirit of dancers in South America

Since both Beatrice and Chase were influential in their particular spheres, they were invited to meet people of importance in the countries they visited: doctors, educators, entrepreneurs, politicians, generals, and kings.

Consider her account of the arrival of King Paul to Kastoria in Greece. "The King arrived after about three-quarters of an hour, piloting his own plane. He is tall, good-looking, about forty-eight, was in uniform and inspected the troops. His appearance is very Nordic. He was introduced and shook hands with each of us. Then immediately he jumped into a waiting Jeep, again driving himself, and went over the roads to the village.

"The roads were lined with enthusiastic peasants as well as troops. As he moved toward headquarters, their enthusiasm became so great that they picked him up, Jeep and all, and carried him through the town."

When, at a later date, Beatrice and Chase met his wife, Queen Frederika of Greece, they were immediately impressed by her energy and involvement. She did express concern that her husband was too reckless, both in his driving and in his daily habits, causing everyone great concern for his safety. He apparently had no sense of fear. The Queen explained to them the difficulty which Greek men have in accepting a woman, and she told them that "each time that she is introduced by her husband, he insists upon having her greeted first." The peasants rather resented the attention, which her husband insisted upon according her, because they considered her "a mere woman."

Beatrice responded appreciatively to most of the places she visited including Rodenburg, Germany, where she enthused over the magnificent stained glass and wood carving in the cathedral, which dated from the Middle Ages. But she was also delighted by the town and its everyday life. In her diary, she recorded, "Along the streets quaint mirrors are attached to the front windows where the ladies could look into them and see when their neighbors went out, who went up and down the street and when they came home, but who themselves sat demurely behind the curtains and although seeing, could not be seen."

After the charm of the village, Beatrice was shocked by the devastation that greeted her in Frankfurt. She remembered the city vividly from an earlier visit and saw that it looked like a nightmare. But nothing prepared her for the great desolation and the ruins of Berlin: "There was rubble, shambles with men and women, figures walking or bicycling, humans furtively looking for cigarette butts and grass overgrowing what was once beautiful parkways and parks. A picture of hopelessness that grips one."

While in Berlin, Beatrice and Chase were invited to a fashion show given by a haute couture. She wrote that 170 models were presented, "each one more elaborate and fashionable than the last. There was, of course, a barrage of private cars as well as those of both the English and American embassies, and we watched for one-half hour the utterly faked picture of plenty parade past."

Shortly after leaving the event, she visited a sort of Women's Exchange where she bought a few dolls for the grandchildren at home. But this was one of the few truly bright spots in her visit to what she referred to as "this isolated island called Berlin."

Two days later, Beatrice and Chase were in Wiesbaden, where George Auerbach and his siblings had lived and gone to school as children. Beatrice found herself "mad and depressed" about the impact the Americans had on Germany. "So much depends upon the result of our ability to change these stubborn people, not by command but by persuasion, and because we have turned the government back to the Germans, we can no longer do anything but offer suggestions and God knows, the Germans, who have been given power, have no objection to our paying for their things, but when it comes to their accepting our leadership, that is no more possible than when the Kaiser ruled or Hitler told them to obey."

She drew an important lesson from what she observed of the dilemma: "I am convinced that we cannot move even though we are not appreciated and it is only lip service of appreciation that we are being given. We must remain there. We must in order for those people to truly feel and know what democracy is-or fail and see Communism take over."

Many of the places she visited merited virtual encomia of praise. Of Zanzibar, she said that it felt as if it came "right out of the pages of romance, intrigue, and a whole storybook of adventures around each turn in the road." This view was bolstered by a visit to the Sultan's Palace, which included the slave cellars, as well as spectacular vistas of the blue and green sea, the coffee plantations, coconut groves, and clove farms.

In Calcutta, they were fascinated by "a temple where sterile wives go to pray for sons and when the prayers are granted, back they go with the navel cord and hang it on the tree above the altar (there are thousands of the cords there) where goats are sacrificed."

In 1953, when Beatrice was nearing her sixty-sixth birthday, she and Chase took a remarkable three-month trip to Africa. On June 7, 1953, a plane took Chase and Beatrice over Victoria Falls. Beatrice was ecstatic. "All my life I have been hearing of the wonder of Victoria Falls before and although often under these conditions the reality is disappointing, this time the reality was far beyond my expectations . . . . It is the most inspiring sight I have ever witnessed and, as I remember Niagara, there is no comparison."

One of their early stops was Ibaden, Nigeria, the largest African city. Beatrice noted, "It has five hundred thousand native Africans and there is no plan and it is ugly and really made of mud and straw."

More than elsewhere, in Africa the travelers confronted delays, cancellations, and alterations of plan. On May 8, they were scheduled to fly first-class from Accra, Ghana, to Lagos in Nigeria. But their flight was cancelled so they had to travel in a "Mammy" plane. The passengers were "all natives, and they travel with their pots, kettles, bundles, and have been known to cook their food in charcoal braziers in the aisle." The plane, a British Marathon, required piling all the luggage up front. There was no attendant on the plane, but they did arrive safely, though later than expected.

On a drive into the backcountry, they were joined by a native chief who decided to honor Beatrice and Chase. He sent his servant back to his house for a gift, and Beatrice observed, "It was interesting to see the servant kneel while receiving instructions in the Cha tribal language." The gift turned out to be a bottle of Black & White Scotch.

Once in the interior, they came to a town they suspected would become the center of an uprising. "Nationalism is the big question," Beatrice wrote, "and although the natives are years away from it, the country is rife with wily politicians many of whom are more interested in their personal aggrandizement than in their country's welfare. So what will happen is anyone's guess."

Moving on to Durban, South Africa, Beatrice observed that "the natives' instincts and habits are nomadic, their intelligence at the present time of a kind that you cannot compare to anything else and even with the greatest sympathy for minorities, one would be foolish to believe that you can jump the years of tribal life as they live it with all their superstitions and witchcraft." In a certain part of the city, monkeys were protected; "they scamper around something like our squirrels do at home and . . . must be equally as great a nuisance."

After visiting South Africa's Zululand, where they were surprised at the eroded soil and washed-out roads, Chase and Beatrice headed for Pretoria. En route, they realized that their passports and tickets had been lost somewhere along the way. Before they could continue their journey, Beatrice and Chase had to obtain replacement visas for Zanzibar, Kenya, Tanganyika, and the Belgian Congo. They also were forced to repeat vaccinations against yellow fever and smallpox. A scramble ensued, but American Express and the consulate were very helpful, and they were able to depart on schedule.

Beatrice described a trip through the Mao Mao country in Kenya, from Nakura, to Thomson's Falls. Stopping to have a meal at the Barry Hotel, she saw that they were the only "people in the dining room without guns in holsters. The people usually carry knives besides. I am a fatalist, as you know, but being completely unarmed as we were certainly gave me a queer feeling."

She defined the Mao Mao as "a secret society which has as its aim to drive the white man out of Kenya . . . . It is nearer the Ku Klux Klan than anything I know, and it originated because of lack of land for the Kikuya and discontent because they consider the white settlers in the highlands have all the best land."

On the Fourth of July, the travelers picnicked at the home of Kenya's consul general and watched Chaplin's *Limelight*.

After a change in schedules, Chase and Beatrice arrived in Khartoum, Sudan, which was dirty, hot, and insect infested. Since no one knew they were coming, they had to fend for themselves at the airport and hotel. They were met with a sandstorm, however, which blocked any sightseeing.

On the journeys Beatrice and Chase took, there always were some harrowing experiences. At a game reserve in Tysavo, Kenya, Beatrice recounted her attempt to photograph a rhinoceros: "I would have taken a magnificent picture, only before I could focus the camera the rhino started charging and Mrs. Bates (our driver) quickly put her foot on the accelerator and we leaped forward at forty miles an hour, the rhinoceros almost keeping abreast." Eventually they lost sight of the rhino, but Beatrice said, "I was so angry at their spoiling my best picture that I had not quite realized what had occurred." Several miles farther on, they heard what they thought was a sawmill, but instead "we perceived millions and millions of locusts actually darkening the sky, and when they landed on the trees, they ate all the green leaves so rapidly that the trees turned instantly from green to dark brown."

Beatrice described a frightening trip on a ten-passenger plane flying to the Belgian Congo where the plane landed on a small plateau: "As you descend, you see precipices on both sides, and heaven help you if the pilot miscalculates by a foot or more, or the wind blows extra hard." This landing was followed immediately by a bus trip, which "careened and swung down the curved road (not paved)," after which they were more than happy to reach their small but comfortable hotel.

On an earlier trip in 1949, Beatrice and Chase were delayed in a Greek seaport town "because of the captain of the small boat being dead drunk and unable to navigate." An old Coast Guard boat with its guns still manned was commandeered to transport the women to Macronissos. But they had to sit in the wheelhouse, and since the seas were rough, they had to close the windows to prevent the spray coming in. The hour-long journey, she noted, "proved our sea stamina."

On the same trip, after enjoying a dinner with King Paul of Greece, she recalled they were on the way back to their billet when they were stopped by a sentry who had not been informed of who they were. He stepped in front of their vehicle "with a gun, his finger on the trigger, pointed directly at us. I assure you it was no idle gesture!" At last, the sentry was persuaded to call his superior officer, and eventually they were allowed to proceed.

Most of their journeys were smooth, but on a trip to the Middle East, Chase and Beatrice arrived without being met at the airport. So they decided to take a taxi driven by a taxi driver who spoke only Arabic and who whisked them away on a one-hundred-mile journey across the desert. "Human lives meant nothing to him," Beatrice recalled, seeing pedestrians jump off the road to avoid the speeding cab.

After the taxi struck a camel and sideswiped a horse, Beatrice decided she'd better try to slow him down. She gestured downward with her hand, but the driver interpreted her message as urging him to *step on it*. "We never stopped bouncing," she recalled.[4]

At tiny Usembura, in the Belgian Congo, they were forced to spend three days "because the road going north is so narrow that they alternate the traffic, sending it 'one way' north on one day, and south the following one."

Chase and Beatrice were always aware of the position of women in the countries they visited. In Usembura, they saw women working in the fields "without clothes except a loin cloth and all use one implement, a hoe of primitive design . . . whatever the purpose." They also saw native women carrying loads of wood on their backs "that would be too much for a donkey."

Their trip to Usembura required them to hire a car and driver. They were presented with an opportunity to advocate for women by hiring a female driver. "We decided that although we had misgivings about a woman chauffeur, if we didn't give her a chance, why should a man?"

Of all the experiences they had in Africa, none matched their visit to the centennial exhibition honoring Cecil Rhodes. Beatrice was bowled over. She wrote, "I am only sorry that our time here was so short. The mining industries, gold, diamond, copper, each have buildings, also the coal and chrome mines . . . . All the countries of Africa (are) represented each with its own building showing the development of the natural resources . . . the development of the natives and the large part the missionaries have had in this . . ." The women expressed regret that their two days there were not enough "to understand what makes these countries tick." Beatrice exclaimed, "What a continent and what a genius Rhodes!" So taken with Rhodes's story was she that she urged her friends and family to read more about him and "never will we be discouraged again, never will we fear . . ."[5]

Chase, who died on December 12, 1984, lived to eulogize her friend Beatrice with whom she had shared so many rich experiences.

Chase Going Woodhouse was one of an elite few in Beatrice's inner circle. Another was Judge Solomon Elsner. When asked about their relationship, Judge Elsner's son James said simply, "He was her legal advisor." Certainly Sol was omnipresent at events in the business community, often appearing as Beatrice's escort after George had died. This led to some speculation that "Judge Elsner and the woman he represented talked the same language . . . They had great affection for one another." When told that the companionship was described by many as "a Spencer Tracy-Katherine Hepburn relationship," his son Morton commented, "My father came home every night."[6]

A handful of letters cast light on the closeness between them. Most of the letters from Judge Elsner bear the salutation "dearest," and many were hand delivered. In a letter dated December 25, 1949, Sol acknowledged the holiday gifts Beatrice had sent and her own handwritten notes accompanying them. He went on, "And all the rest, darling, are in my heart—gratefulness, solicitude, yearning, caring, love." Then he wrote, "When the heart speaks, the mind closes. It has so much to say . . . . I know, however, that we do understand for the organs which are called our hearts have now been attuned over all the years." In April 1950, he wrote, "It is seldom we are alone together, and the few times we are these days are always the heartening and sustaining facets in my present existence." In that same letter, he addressed her as "darling" and "sweetheart," strongly suggesting a relationship that went beyond the professional or the merely friendly. Others who have commented on the nature of the bond between Beatrice and

Solomon said that if theirs was a romance, they were very discreet, primarily out of consideration for Mrs. Elsner. For her part, Beatrice's letters addressed to him often bore the salutation "Sol, dear." On her many trips abroad, when writing home to her loved ones, she always included Sol. In one letter, she wrote to her daughters: "I hope you are loving Sol (in spite of himself)."

Certainly, there was much to draw them together besides the business connection. Judge Elsner (even when he was no longer a judge, he was always referred to by that title) had known Beatrice since childhood. In fact, according to Margery Hartman Oakes, the daughter of Beatrice's best friend Estelle Hartman, in youth, Beatrice and Sol wanted to marry, but her parents would not give their consent. In his letters to Beatrice before their marriage, George expressed gratitude that Sol and the Hartmans squired her to social events in his absence. He claimed no jealousy, but he wanted her to reassure him that her devotion was solely to him. In one extant postcard from her cousin Blanche to Beatrice at Benjamin Deane School dated October 21, 1905, a photo of Vanderbilt Hall at Yale was circled with the caption, "Sol's room."

Solomon Elsner's grandparents emigrated from Bohemia, hers from Germany, and they had been raised with similar values. "They saw their Jewishness as an important part of their cultural orientation. Yet they also wanted to be accepted as Connecticut Yankees."[7]

Some of her business decisions seemed to have been encouraged by Judge Elsner who shared Beatrice's devotion to the city of Hartford. Among these were the building of the G. Fox parking garage in the 1950s, even though the beginnings of middle-class exodus from the city were already evident. Sol also encouraged Beatrice to take a leadership role in the creation of Constitution Plaza as a mecca for visitors and patrons alike. As a longtime member of the Hartford Redevelopment Agency, Sol believed that converting a slumlike section of the city into a thriving and handsome business center would be of significant benefit to G. Fox as well.

Beatrice's faith in the city of Hartford was strongly evident in her direction of G. Fox itself. Other department stores, like Sage-Allen and Lord & Taylor, were rapidly opening satellites. She refused to allow suburban branches to be built because she feared they would "dilute the excellence of Fox's" and its position as a vital center. There were two exceptions to this rule. One was a pharmacy branch at Hartford Hospital, and the other was Foxmart, located in South Windsor and designed as a facility to service rural customers. The merchandise included barn, dairy, and farm equipment. Sol Elsner was the prime mover in establishing Foxmart, believing that the Connecticut agricultural community was an underserved market. The Foxmart experiment lasted only a few years and was a financial failure, something rare for Mrs. Auerbach. Some people laid the blame for the unsuccessful venture on Sol's advice.[8] As her frequent escort to business and community events, he was recognized as a significant force, having the ear and the trust of one of Hartford's most powerful citizens.

As much as Beatrice trusted Sol, one exception to her dependence on his advice is documented in a correspondence concerning the disposition of 1,745 shares of Standard Trust company stock, which formed part of the estate of Moses Fox. Moses died in 1938, and these letters are dated 1940 and 1941.

One item is a detailed summary of the holdings in the estate and the current status of the investments. It was prepared by Sol Elsner and attached to a memo covering three or four business issues. Apparently, Fan wanted to sell the stock and divide the proceeds. She wanted Beatrice to set a date when she could have the portion of her father's holdings that should come to her.

Beatrice chose to respond to Fan without showing the letter to Sol because he would hit the ceiling at what she proposed to do. Beatrice told Fan she was wrong to "assert rights which you never had, but which you assumed only because of my wish that, regardless of the burden to me, you were to have one-half of Dad's remaining Standard stock." Sol had pointed out that Standard's Board of Directors could have sold the stock by majority vote without Fan's consent, and Beatrice said she regretted the lack of trust in her that "raises all the rim." She assured Fan that she planned to tell Sol she wanted to get her own affairs in order and would ask him "to promptly find a way of getting the Standard stock out of the estate so that it can be divided and transferred into our names." She added, "You can take this assurance that long before September 1, 1943, you will have your stock."

In yet another letter, Beatrice said she didn't want to get "all stirred up, hot and bothered" over the Standard issue. "So let's just forget it. Know that it is not a matter of right that is being recognized, but a matter of my deep love and consideration for you." Certainly, she wanted nothing and no one, not even Sol, to disturb the devoted relationship she and Fan always shared.

On the day Judge Elsner died, April 18, 1962, Anne Uccello, who regularly reviewed advertisements in the New York papers to keep current with what was being featured in the city stores, was called to Beatrice's office. Ms. Uccello said, "She asked to review the papers with me, but I believe she really wanted me there to divert her attention from her loss."

Another close friend was Eleanor Roosevelt. Beatrice did not spend as much time with her as she did with Sol or Chase, but there was an ongoing correspondence beginning in 1946 and continuing until Eleanor's death in 1962. They were drawn together because both were women of importance, both were widows, and both led singularly busy lives. But more than that, they shared ideas and ideals. Beatrice hoped to achieve through the Women's Service Bureau an awareness of national and international issues, particularly as they affected women, or, as women could affect them.

The friendship began in 1946 when Beatrice invited Eleanor to speak at the October meeting of the Service Bureau. Eleanor responded that she could not, explaining, "The UN Assembly will be in session and I cannot make any other engagements." Her commitment to the United Nations was chronicled often in their correspondence.

Eventually, Mrs. Roosevelt did speak to the Service Bureau in December of 1947. After her visit, Beatrice wrote, "(I) am sure you will be interested in knowing that there were 101 towns of Connecticut represented at the meeting, which is in itself a great compliment as Connecticut women are not of the meeting type." In this statement, Beatrice revealed why she was so anxious to have the Service Bureau educate women and strengthen their role in their community and nation. She knew that in many ways, hers was an uphill battle.

Beatrice, Chase, and Eleanor Roosevelt

Many of the letters between Beatrice and Eleanor consisted of invitations to Eleanor to spend time in Connecticut or for Beatrice to join Eleanor for lunch or dinner or a reception. Since Beatrice kept an apartment in New York, it was possible for her to visit Eleanor in the city, though often only for an hour or two. In 1950, Beatrice extended the first of several invitations to Eleanor to spend the weekend at Auerfarm "at a time when we could also enjoy going up to the Berkshire Festival at Tanglewood." The sojourn would "afford you some degree of relaxation," she added.

Eleanor did, in fact, visit at Auerfarm and at
1040 Prospect Avenue a few times over the years.
In a syndicated column written at Hyde Park on
July 28, 1951, Eleanor described one visit:

A more perfect place for a busy woman I cannot
imagine. Mrs. Auerbach can be at her office in
Hartford in fifteen minutes, and when she returns
to the farm, she is in complete wilderness.

The cabins are set among the trees, and when the
sun filters through in the morning, it is a sight to
behold. Around my cabin were many white birches,
and I could just glimpse below in the hollow the
blue sheen of the water in the swimming pool.[9] I
felt quite at home, for only screens surrounded my
bedroom, the windows having been taken out for
the summer. Breakfast on the porch in the morning
was deliciously cool and quiet.

Mrs. Auerbach's son-in-law took us for a tour
of the farm. Their chicken business is wonderfully
run, and they have a minimum of fifteen thousand
chickens all the time. I marvel at the machinery, which
makes it possible to use a minimum of manpower.

Their dairy is wonderful indeed, Guernseys like
ours, and they sell whole milk, cream, and cottage
cheese. They pasteurize and bottle their own milk

and run a milk route. They have bought some bulls and are shortly going to begin selling purebred stock for breeding purposes.

They do not, however, grow enough feed for their needs, so they are trying to reclaim some of their land. When that is accomplished, it seems to me that this farm should be on a paying basis.[10]

On June 7, 1951, Mrs. Roosevelt had been on hand at Centinel Hill Hall to open an exhibit of paintings done by Sylvia Patricelli whom she had encouraged Mrs. Auerbach to befriend and to advise about how to get her work exhibited. Ms. Patricelli, an Australian who married an American, was recommended to Eleanor by Lady Gowrie, the wife of the governor of New South Wales and a noted philanthropist in her own right. Especially interested in the encouragement of young artists, Lady Gowrie urged Eleanor to do whatever she could to help Ms. Patricelli. When Eleanor first solicited Beatrice's assistance, in November of 1950, Beatrice responded, "I hope that I can be helpful, particularly because of your interest." She referred to the artist as Mrs. Roosevelt's protégée and arranged an exhibit of her work in the G. Fox auditorium.

Mrs. Auerbach extended a special invitation to members of the Centinel Hill Teen Club to hear Mrs. Roosevelt speak. Mrs. Roosevelt's message was powerful, stressing the importance of teenagers in America reaching out to other countries. "Senator McCarthy has made us a timid nation," she said. "I would rather see us make mistakes than be afraid." She worried that "our young people today are eager to be conservative, on the safe side, rather than new or daring in their opinions." She predicted that, "We are going to have to send young people—the girls and boys of today—into the rest of the world, and they will have to learn languages and learn them quickly."[11]

On June 8, 1951, (the day following the speech) Beatrice expressed to Eleanor her concern about the audience. "Am really worried about the teenagers because a club of over five hundred members had the rare opportunity of listening to you and yet did not take advantage of it. It fills me with fear for our youth, and am really disturbed and caused to wonder why. The principals of the schools the girls attend were all there, I noticed, but there was a sparseness in the number of girls themselves. It is unfathomable to me."

In August of 1951, Beatrice wrote to Eleanor asking if she had any suggestions about people she and Chase might visit while in India. Eleanor responded with a couple of names and offered to write letters of introduction for the travelers. Judging from her correspondence, Beatrice had often obtained letters of introduction from individuals and from the Department of State. This pattern was followed on several trips to various parts of the world that would be an important part of Beatrice's life. Beatrice, too, in her correspondence with Eleanor, made some specific suggestions to her globe-hopping friend. On March 1, 1952, Beatrice wrote, "Do hope the trip to Kashmir is going to be part of your itinerary because reading and talking to people about it is not like seeing it." It turned out that Eleanor could not visit Kashmir because she had to be in New York for the Human Rights Commission.

In July of 1952, Beatrice was invited to visit Eleanor at her New York apartment at a time when Eleanor's family were in attendance. Beatrice wrote to her, "It is always a privilege and pleasure to see you with your grandchildren and the young people, and am sure that they will never forget your wonderful influence and love for them." Beatrice here was reflecting on a high priority for both women. In spite of their extraordinarily busy lives, spending time with family was of great importance to them. Knowing how important her family was to Beatrice, Eleanor even included Beatrice's grandchildren, Rena and George Koopman, in an invitation to a New Year's Eve party at her apartment.

On another occasion, in the fall of 1952, Beatrice confirmed plans for luncheon and asked Eleanor if she could arrange to have Ralph Bunche join them. Beatrice was especially keen to meet him because "here at the store, we have been doing considerable work in initiating the minority race into the allover picture in retailing, and I have been the springboard for it." This was one of the few times Beatrice claimed credit for one of what would be a number of initiatives to advance those who are disadvantaged because of race, ethnicity, or gender. With some humility and no little frustration, Beatrice told Eleanor that Mr. Bunche's secretary seemed to protect him from "ordinary contacts such as mine." And though Eleanor made an effort to bring Mr. Bunche to the table, she offered her regrets that she must disappoint Beatrice since she had not been successful in luring him.

On November twenty-sixth of 1955, Beatrice wrote to Eleanor about a "disastrous fire at the farm" the week before. All the main buildings of the farm were burned. To add to her distress, she revealed that her longtime chauffeur, Harry Ronan, had passed away. Beatrice remarked that she really felt "that the people who serve us are nearer than one's friends for they see us under all kinds of circumstances—not only when we are ready to meet the world but when we are not as well." She said that, although she had much to be thankful for, "this Thanksgiving made me feel a wee bit sorry for myself."

Eleanor responded immediately, saying, "No wonder you felt a wee bit sorry. However, I know what a wonderful spirit you have, and I am sure you are already beginning to see the brighter side of things." Indeed, she assumed correctly. The farm was rebuilt under the direction of Beatrice's son-in-law, Richard Koopman, using the most modern equipment available. Farmers came from around New England to marvel at the completed project.

In August of 1958, Eleanor communicated to Beatrice her intention of leaving her apartment on E. Sixty-second Street because "they decided to raise my rent to such a ridiculous price that I just wouldn't pay it." Apparently, neither woman was to be coerced into foolish expense. Time and again, as evident in her notes in travel diaries, Beatrice is modest in her needs; and although she and Chase sometimes enjoyed sumptuous accommodations, she could adjust as well to the most basic of conditions, concerning herself with what was needed without expectation of more.

Among their correspondence was a series of letters, beginning in 1958, that the family referred to as "the egg letters." Addressing Beatrice as "my dear friend," Eleanor thanked her for the dozen eggs from Auerfarm that Beatrice had had delivered to her in New York by her chauffeur. Eleanor wrote, "I am enchanted by your gifts."[12] In a subsequent letter, after many references to gifts of eggs, Eleanor wrote that these eggs really came in handy when, on the way to fly to Chicago, she was forced to return home because weather prohibited takeoff. When she arrived home, she found that her maid had taken the night off, so Eleanor "raided the icebox and had a wonderful time frying bacon with an egg. It was a fine and satisfying meal."

In June of 1959, Beatrice wrote, "As usual you are looking just wonderful. I marvel at how you do the many things as well as give joy to so many people by giving of yourself and still keep looking well and ready for whatever blows come your way—and know many do. After being with you, (I) always feel stronger in my determination to make some kind of a contribution to the world in which we are living."

In April 1960, Eleanor injured her ankle. So Beatrice sent her chauffeur to bring Eleanor up to Hartford and sent a letter to Eleanor's secretary urging her to persuade Eleanor to bring her along because that would "add to her comfort and convenience while she is here." Eleanor would have none of that, and she even arranged to speak to the Service Bureau women while she was in Hartford.

Several months later, while on a trip to South America with Chase Woodhouse, Beatrice penned a lengthy letter to Eleanor, which included a description of her trip home from Peru. She pointed out, "I had better return to Hartford ready to work and not for a rest cure . . . . The Santa Luisa is sailing with thirteen passengers, six of whom are youngsters, two ourselves, and the five others not interesting enough for us to remain awake and active. Therefore, it's a long, long rest which it is doubtful if I'll ever have patience enough to repeat, but certainly is good for one to do once in twenty years." Noting that it was Eleanor's birthday that week, Beatrice wished her "many, many years to come with health so that you can do as much for so many humans as you continually do. Wisdom, inspiration so that you inspire the devotion and the determination to follow your unselfish leadership. There are so few people as one gathers the years that mean friendship or rather new ones as the years go on. So you are dear friend a rare, rare person, and God certainly did destroy the mold after you were created."

In 1960, Beatrice wrote about a luncheon with Eleanor and a lady from California who amused them by admitting she had been in vaudeville, and that she was en route to pick up her new Rolls Royce. Beatrice said, "Life certainly does bring many funny circumstances, and it can be lots of fun if one takes it all with a sense of humor. That you are able to do and hope I can emulate you in that one phase of your life at least."

In a letter of June 18, 1960, after a trip to Hartford where Eleanor gave another talk for the

Service Bureau, Beatrice wrote, "You must have been dead tired when you reached home, and I do hope this week will bring you a little respite from your strenuous activities. May I tell you that you were superb the other night, and you gave me much food for thought. In fact, yesterday I had to speak to and spend time with a number of our older employees who are retiring under our pension plan. Between what they get from the store pension and their Social Security, they really have no financial worries in their old age, but they have not been educated in the fact that they can now use their time to do for others."

She went on to tell Eleanor about her attendance at the graduation of the American School for the Deaf, an institution in which Beatrice took a significant interest. "When one sees these young men and women so terrifically handicapped, it makes one realize more than ever that guidance cannot be left to chance, but we are in a way responsible."

In June of 1962, Beatrice admonished Eleanor, "Never (to) let anyone tell you that you are not every bit as you were ten or fifteen years ago. As a matter of fact, there has come with it greater maturity and greater, greater wisdom, and we all benefit from it." A few months later, on hearing that Eleanor had been unable to fight off a "pesky bug" and would go to Campobello to rest and recover, Beatrice wrote, "It is too bad that as we grow older, the ability to stretch our strength leaves us, and I know I find it so in my own case. However, there is so much to do that one hates to let down." Once again, the commitment of each of these two women to addressing social problems was contained in what proved to be the final letter Beatrice would write to Eleanor.

On November 8, 1962, Mrs. Roosevelt succumbed to her illness, and at the request of the Roosevelt family, Beatrice was invited to her internment ceremony at Hyde Park on November 10, 1962.[13]

THE FINAL CHAPTER

In September of 1963, Mrs. Auerbach received an inquiry about the possibility of renewing negotiations to affiliate G. Fox with Federated Department Stores. When first approached years earlier, Mrs. Auerbach was not interested in pursuing the matter, and she responded that it would be up to her children to do what they wanted to do after she was gone.

According to Ira Neimark, in 1963, Beatrice seriously considered affiliating with Federated, but they overextended their acquisitions. In 1965, Mrs. Auerbach announced that G. Fox was to be "joined with the May Company." The terms *merged*, *bought*, or *sold* were never used in reference to the transition. And she insisted that the merchandise management remain the same. Consistent with her management style, Beatrice prepared a detailed explanation of the move for the store's employees. The message she delivered personally from the Mezzanine to a gathering of employees on the main floor of the store was reproduced in the *Go-Getter* for October 27, 1965.

> I have called you together because I want to talk with you personally, as I always have when there is a matter of mutual importance and concern. This is our store. It has been in the family 118 years. It is a part of each of us. From our earliest days to the present, PEOPLE—our employees and customers—have been most important to us. Together with you, we have brought the store to the present high reputation in the community, the state, and even the nation. We have made a contribution to the growth and revitalization of the community as we expanded our store in downtown Hartford. We have been told that we have been a stimulant and example for higher ethical standards of business in this area. We always have had a deep-rooted belief in the dignity of the individual and have conducted

our business lives in such a way as to win the respect of our customers and the support and understanding of our employees.

As a business develops and grows, there comes a time when certain decisions have to be made. Such decisions as "Do we stand still?" "Do we advance slowly?" or "Do we move forward in a vigorous manner?" We have worked together for many years, and you know we have not "stood still." Although we have been vigorous and vital, the time has arrived for an even more vigorous thrust forward—that should mean greater and wider expansion of G. Fox & Co., new growth, and with it even fuller opportunities for each of us.

How to accomplish these objectives, how to ensure the continuance of the standards that are ours, how to ensure the things G. Fox & Co., has and must continue to stand for, has for a long time, been a matter of serious discussion and concern to me and my family.

We have come to an important decision to ensure this necessary progress for our organization, its employees, and its public. We believe the best way of doing this is to join with an outstanding Store Group—one that can contribute to us as we can contribute to it. That group is the May Department Stores Company. They too have grown from a family institution to an organization of many fine stores.

In this association, the business of our store will continue to be conducted by me and my family. Merchandising standards, service standards, personnel standards, and integrity will continue as always. As a part of this continuity, I have been asked, and expressed my willingness, to be a May Department Stores Co. director. The members of my family will also be intimately and importantly involved.

The deep concern that I have inherited from my father for your welfare will not change. I shall be here running our business, along with the family and executives who have stood so faithfully at my side for so many years, to assure all of you that Fox's is going forward as the unique store that we are and always will be.

There are many questions that you will ask and many things you will want to know more about that will be answered. But it was important to me that I personally tell you what the future holds. The future holds nothing but good for all of us as long as we have faith in one another.

An early result of the transfer of power was the opening of a number of G. Fox branch stores at area shopping malls. The acquisition of G. Fox positioned May as a growing national chain. "The prestigious reputation of G. Fox enhanced May's quest for an upscale image. G. Fox's $60 million volume increased May's annual volume by 10 percent."[1]

The May Company acquired Filene's of Boston in 1988. With twenty stores and an annual volume over $500 million, Filene's became the flagship of May's fleet. In 1993, the G. Fox store in downtown Hartford closed its doors, and the Fox name at thirteen regional branches was changed to Filene's.[2]

Why Beatrice chose to relinquish control of G. Fox is a matter of some debate. Her secretary, Shirley Koplowitz, said she believed that Mrs. Auerbach realized the changes that were likely in the near future, but uppermost in her mind was the wish to divide the business equally between the Koopmans and the Schiros, thus avoiding any possible contention within the family. Beatrice told an interviewer, Linda Case, "I merged because I wanted to give my family a freedom of action in doing what they wanted in life."[3]

But it is also true that the tax structure had made it nearly impossible to continue ownership of the store as a private family concern because passing the business down to another generation would be taxed at a rate of 50 percent of total worth. According to Richard Koopman, the tax would have prevented the family maintaining the level of service that was traditional for G. Fox.

As part of the agreement with May, Beatrice remained president for one year; and in 1966, she named Richard Koopman president and Bernard Schiro chairman. In her remaining years, she concentrated her energies on philanthropic pursuits.

Beatrice Fox Auerbach died on November 29, 1968, at Hartford Hospital, a victim of congestive heart failure. Her funeral was the largest ever held in Hartford for a private citizen, and it was attended by dignitaries from in and outside the state, leaders of all religious faiths, friends, acquaintances, and employees. The services were conducted at Beth Israel Temple by rabbis Abraham Feldman and Harold Silver. The *Hartford Times* and the *Hartford Courant* as well as leading newspapers in the other cities and towns of Connecticut eulogized her as one of the most influential figures in the history of the state.

Among those whose comments were cited was Mrs. Chase Going Woodhouse who said of her friend, "Mrs. Auerbach believed in the ability of the people of Connecticut to uphold our traditions of work, tolerance, and mutual neighborly help and to build a continuing better way of life.

"To that end, she gave not only generous material aid but also time, a creative mind, and friendship to assist our schools, universities, and our women's organizations to work toward this goal. Her life typifies what Thomas Jefferson described as the American citizen, essential to maintain our national standards and our democracy."[4]

Arthur J. Lamsden, president of the Greater Hartford Chamber of Commerce, said, "It is hard to imagine Hartford without her. All the good work she has done has made Hartford a better place to live for everybody."[5]

Governor John Dempsey marked her passing as the loss of "Hartford's leading citizen and true first lady."[6]

Leaders of religious organizations such as Rabbi Feldman; the Catholic archbishop of Hartford, Henry J. O'Brien; and the Rt. Rev. Walter H. Gray, Episcopal bishop of Connecticut, each expressed appreciation for her extraordinary tolerance and charitable spirit. As Bishop Gray put it, "She was genuinely concerned with people and always ready to help in anything she believed in. She was intelligent in her religious life and appreciative of people of other faiths."[7]

George J. Minnery, chairman of the Retail Trade Board, called Mrs. Auerbach "a great humanitarian. A great lady and a great competitor . . . . The key word in her store was *integrity*." Pomeroy Day, CEO of Connecticut Bank and Trust Company, said, "We can be proud that she lived among us. She represented the highest ideals."[8]

Chairman of the Hartford Development Commission, E. Clayton Gengras, observed, "With

Mrs. Auerbach's death, Hartford loses one of its most devoted and dedicated citizens—a person who will live forever. And she will be greatly missed. If you would see her monument, just look around you."[9]

Her burial vault is located in Beth Israel Cemetery on Ward Street in Hartford. She rests a few yards from her parents and her lifelong friends, the Hartmans.

In addition to major gifts to the Jewish community, Beatrice left one-third of her estate to the Beatrice Fox Auerbach Foundation, which was designed to continue supporting education, arts, and worthy causes in the city and the state. Eventually, Georgette and Dorothy elected to have the funds folded into the Hartford Foundation for Public Giving, which to this day continues to support some of the many causes close to the heart of Beatrice herself.

Epilogue

The life of Beatrice Fox Auerbach is a testimony to her entrepreneurial and philanthropic achievements. She supported an array of causes with her time and her money.

In a Producers Guild playbill, acknowledging her sponsorship, this phrase appears: "her legacy is scattered around Hartford like sprinkled goodness." Indeed, Beatrice was instrumental in the success of a number of causes. One way to capture the breadth of her generosity is to examine how many different entities benefited from her largesse.

Beatrice welcomed any opportunity to advocate for Jews. Until the 1950s, the only hospital in Hartford was Hartford Hospital, serving the entire community. (Later, St. Francis Hospital would be built to serve the Catholic community, and

Mount Sinai for the Jewish community.) Stephen B. Goddard, a reporter for the *Hartford Times*, shared a story told to him by his father. When Beatrice was asked to contribute to Hartford Hospital, she wrote to Dr. Goddard asking to see the personnel roster. After reviewing it, she told Dr. Goddard that he should contact her again when at least two Jewish interns were on the staff. As a community leader, Beatrice was often invited to meetings on civic affairs. When they were held at the Hartford Club, a major gathering place in the city, she refused to attend because the club was not open to Jews.

Education was of primary importance to Beatrice as reflected in the endowment of a retailing major at Connecticut College for Women and in the Service Bureau for Women's Organizations. The Service Bureau was well established by the time Beatrice was no longer able to participate in its programs. A glance at the sort of topics taken up by the organization after her death confirms the continued relevance of its purpose. In 1970, the bureau worked again with problems associated with aging. Ever practical, they included architects speaking on housing design for the elderly. And at the annual legislative forum conducted by the bureau, Dr. LeRoy Wardner of Hartford Hospital discussed legislation concerning abortion in a workshop on population control.

In 1972, the group took an active role assisting in the establishment of group homes for women. They sought to provide educational and vocational training for females ages sixteen to twenty-one coming from low-income families in Greater Hartford. The project, sponsored by the Service Bureau and the Job Corps, felt that the experience of living away from home was crucial to the success of these young women.

The Service Bureau represented the pioneering quality of Beatrice's philanthropy. She was ahead of her time in seeking to educate women in leadership positions, and by educating the broader public in the process, she gave an invaluable gift to her city, her state, and her nation. Society has gone a considerable distance to strengthen gender equality since the 1960s, but there can be no gainsaying Beatrice Auerbach's place in the forefront of that effort.

On the campus of the University of Hartford, of which she was a founder, are a lecture hall named Auerbach Auditorium, the Auerbach Computer Center, and Auerbach Hall, a major building

housing the school of business. She was a regular
supporter of the university's Hartt College of
Music, especially the opera program, and of the
Hartford Art School.

**Groundbreaking for Auerbach Hall on the
campus of The University of Hartford, 1966**

She funded scholarships at St. Joseph College,
a Catholic institution for women, the Hartford

Conservatory of Music, the University of Hartford, and the University of Connecticut. In 1956, Beatrice endowed a professorship in economics at Trinity College. All of these institutions, as well as Wesleyan and Hebrew Union College, rewarded her generosity with honorary degrees or citations. The text that accompanied the award of Doctor of Humane Letters, Honoris Causa from the University of Hartford speaks for all.[1]

Distinguished Hartford citizen, wise humanitarian and farseeing businesswoman; faithfully upholding the sterling traditions of a famous Hartford enterprise and centennial institution known throughout the country; you have also found time, beside attending to the heavy press of administrative duties, to further the statewide cause of education, to establish in memory of your father the Moses Fox Club, so that loyal employees may receive their due honors and awards for years of dependable service; to establish and develop the Beatrice Fox Auerbach Foundation and the Service Bureau for Women's Organizations of Connecticut, which, through adult education, has done so much to further a better understanding of national and international relations. Further, as a genuine ambassador of American good will all over Europe this side of the Iron Curtain, you have been instrumental in bringing about the reciprocal evidence of international and democratic good will by facilitating the visits of numbers of Free Europeans who have been entertained in private homes throughout this state. But. far more than all of this, you have privately found opportunity to bring personal attention and inspiriting human sympathy to the suffering and distressed in your immediate vicinity.

In 1955, Beatrice was a delegate to the White House Conference on Education.

Beatrice was generous, too, to the arts in Hartford. Her initial gift to the Wadsworth Atheneum was earmarked for the purpose of refurbishing the library and "to create a space which would hold close to twenty thousand volumes."[2] The space now houses forty-four thousand items. As the plan for the project unfolded, Beatrice recognized that it called for the replacement of the woodwork. She insisted that the oak paneling from the Watkinson Library, dating from the 1860s, be restored instead.

The library was eventually named the Beatrice Fox Auerbach Library. On December 19, 1963, the *Hartford Courant* reported her gift of $200,000.00 in honor of her daughters and sons-in-law. Over a period of years, Georgette Koopman herself contributed several hundred volumes to the museum library.

Beatrice at the Wadsworth Atheneum

Beatrice endowed the conductor's chair for
the Hartford Symphony Orchestra and served on
the symphony's board of directors. Judge James
Kinsella, also a member of the board, recalled a
particularly contentious meeting where Beatrice sat
as an island of calm while others were embroiled
in a high-pitched debate. The judge asked if she
was not going to express her opinion, and Beatrice
replied, "Yes, after they've all calmed down enough
to listen to reason." Her value as a member of the
board of this and other institutions cannot be
overstated. Too often, people who serve on such
boards see the appointment as largely honorary,
and are not fully engaged, but this was never the
case with Beatrice. As Mary Smith put it in her 1985
presentation to the Ladies Club of Cortland, New
York, "Beatrice Auerbach did not contribute to or
espouse causes lightly, and her gifts were generous
and carefully planned. She gave not only of her
money but of her talents and her time . . . . She
had a brilliant analytical mind which she brought
to bear on anything with which she was connected.
Her sense of social responsibility was of the highest
order. She was fiercely proud of her city and
state and always said, 'Our wealth has come from

Connecticut, and it will go back to Connecticut.' Through it all, people were her abiding interest and concern."[3]

While Beatrice, like her entire family, tried to stay out of politics, her influence on civic affairs was considerable. One of the most persistent myths about her claims that, when plans were being made for the connection of Interstate highways 84 and 91 in Hartford, she insisted that the design ensure that all traffic was directed past G. Fox. What appears to be an abuse of power is probably not. The highway connection was part of a much larger plan for urban redevelopment, which would have made the area north of G. Fox residential, a fact which supported the highway configuration that developed.[4] But even if the urban legend about her heavy-handedness was just that—a legend—as Linda Case wrote, "She expounded a variation of the old General Motors pitch: What's good for G. Fox is good for Hartford."[5] A metal casting on her desk at the store read, "If it's good for G. Fox & Company, I'm for it." She was a master at promoting the store and committed to the concept that her department store was, *in fact*, the Center of Connecticut Living.

The Fox and Auerbach families did not, themselves, seek political office. But Beatrice encouraged the candidacy of Anne Uccello, one of her comparison shoppers, for the Hartford City Council. In the Democratic stronghold that was Hartford, the prospect of a Republican woman being elected was not seen as promising.

Ms. Uccello remembers Beatrice saying to her one day during the campaign, "Mark my words. You will be mayor of Hartford." Not only was Ms. Uccello elected to the council, but also by virtue of garnering the highest number of votes, she was named the city's mayor, fulfilling Beatrice's prognostication, and she was the first woman ever to hold that office. She credited Beatrice for giving her the courage to run and remembered the congratulations she got from her boss for "facing down the machine."

The renovation of the downtown store in 1938, when the Depression was not yet a memory, and the revamping of a major parking facility on Market Street in 1950 served to revitalize the downtown area. The observation of Phyllis E. Byer is apropos. "The store was a refuge of tasteful temptation through the Depression and World War II. It was not just the crown jewel of local commerce, but also a center of social life. There were women who spent part of their day in the spacious lounge at the entrance to the glorious pink and gray ladies' room, always assured of encountering a familiar face. And one familiar face, ever present in the store, belonged to Beatrice Fox Auerbach, the store's president, roaming the floors, checking displays, greeting customers, and calling employees by name.[6] No one was surprised that in 1956, the U.S. Chamber of Commerce named her the year's outstanding boss."

The numerous accolades that came to Beatrice, in addition to those mentioned, underscore the extent of her reputation and philanthropic efforts. Among her many awards was the National Human Relations Award given by the Connecticut and Western Massachusetts region of the National Conference of Christians and Jews. Her cohonoree was Jackie Robinson. As an inveterate Dodgers fan, she must have been pleased at that. She was given the Public Service Award by the Connecticut Bar Association in particular to honor her for stimulating interest in international affairs. B'nai B'rith honored her leadership, and the American Legion Auxiliaries

bestowed on Beatrice their Distinguished Service
Award, and she was named Woman of the Year by
Delta Phi Epsilon International Sorority.

Beatrice and Jackie Robinson receive NCCJ Award

Beatrice contributed to the local hospitals, with
gifts ranging from lamps for the surgical floor at
J. J. McCook Hospital to the entire maternity wing

at Hartford Hospital. A regular contributor to the
Connecticut School for the Blind, Beatrice served
on the board of the American School for the Deaf
and was in the forefront of efforts to assist that
institution. But her favorite philanthropic activities
were the many personal and individual gifts she
gave to those in need.

Margery Oakes said that Beatrice led her life in
accordance with Micah chapter 6, verse 8: "He hath
shewed thee, O man, what is good; and what doth
the Lord require of thee but to do justly, and to
love mercy, and to walk humbly with thy God?"

*   *   *

Both Georgette and Dorothy inherited their
mother's dedication to philanthropy. Georgette
was the more active of the two, supporting the
arts, education, and community causes. She had
a particular interest in art. She joined the Board
of Trustees of the Wadsworth Atheneum in 1968,
and she served as a trustee and later an honorary
trustee until her death. She was especially known
for her clarity and decisiveness of mind, as well
as her respect for the opinions of others. The

museum bestowed on her its highest honor, the Goodwin Medal.

For decades, Georgette was a staunch supporter of the Hartford Art School at the University of Hartford. Elected trustee in 1966, she was twice president of the board. Once again, her service was recognized in the granting of the Hartford Art School Medal, an honor given only rarely in the school's history. For eighteen years, Georgette was a member of the Board of Regents of the University of Hartford, receiving the University Medal for Distinguished Service. And as a graduate of the Oxford School, she served on the Board of Trustees of Kingswood/Oxford for nine years.

Like her mother, Georgette was an enthusiastic supporter of the Hartford Symphony Orchestra and the Hartford Stage Company.

A great many institutions in the Hartford area benefited from Georgette's leadership. Among them were the Hebrew Home and Hospital, the Connecticut Institute for the Blind, and the American School for the Deaf—all causes espoused by her mother as well. Georgette was a corporator of the Hartford Hospital and of St. Francis Hospital and Medical Center. She gave time to the United

Way and the Connecticut Valley Girl Scout Council, and the Rotary Club of Hartford honored her with their Vocational Service Award in 2003.

Dorothy's activities, while often quiet or anonymous, spanned a wide variety of civic and educational causes. She was especially interested in the Girl Scouts and the 4-H. For a number of years, Dorothy was coordinator of Girl Scout Cookie Sales for the town of West Hartford. In 1975, she challenged the 4-Hers to make productive the orchard at Auerfarm, where the organization had been granted a home. A $500.00 prize was earmarked for the group should they succeed, which they did.

When honors were offered to Dorothy for her community service, she usually declined saying, "I am not worthy. I haven't done enough yet."[7] At the same time, Dorothy made every effort to see to it that others were recognized for their contributions.

Much of the sisters' philanthropic activity came through funds they both established at the Hartford Foundation for Public Giving, where they guided the distribution of the Beatrice Fox Auerbach Foundation funds as well as endowments established in both the Koopman and Schiro names.

Endnotes

Chapter One

1. *Hartford Courant*, 1/30/17, 1.
2. *Hartford Courant* and *Hartford Daily Times*, 1/30/17-2/3/17 passim.
3. *Hartford Times*, 1/31/17, 9.
4. Ibid.
5. *Hartford Courant*, 1/31/17, 3.
6. Ibid.
7. *Hartford Times*, 2/3/17.

Chapter Two

1. Cited in *A Century in Connecticut*, a publication by G. Fox and Co., commemorating the 100th anniversary.
2. Obituary of Frederick Stern, Newburgh, New York, April 24, 1913.

3   *A Century in Connecticut.*

4. When interviewed, Margery Oakes said that her mother, Estelle Hartman, spoke of this as something Beatrice told her in confidence.

5. In most photographs of Beatrice taken in her childhood and teen years, she wore glasses. In later photos, she always appears without them.

6. Yearbook of the Benjamin Deane School, 1909.

Chapter Three

1. In 1959, Fan and Les Samuels established a foundation to support a variety of causes. In 1981, after forty-one years in New York City, the Samuels decided to target their funds to the betterment of the people of New York. They were major donors to Lincoln Center, giving millions of dollars to the facility and its programs. Other New York arts organizations, large and small, also profited from their generosity. A second mission of the foundation was to support improvements in the health care and overall quality of life of the elderly. Although the Samuels both died more than twenty years ago, the foundation continues to carry on their generosity.

In 2006, the assets of the foundation were $170 million.

2. Exactly who Wallingford was is uncertain. Perhaps the reference is to the Earl of Wallingford who, in the twelfth century, was infamous for his acquisition of lands.

3. Eveline Brooks Auerbach, *Frontier Reminiscences.*

4. Ralph Tannenbaum, "The Jewish Community in Utah," *Utah History Encyclopedia.*

5. Ibid.

6. *New York Times*, April 4, 1911.

7. W, Paul Reeve, *History Blazer,* August, 1995.

8. Ibid.

9. Tannenbaum

Chapter Four

1. It was common practice at the time for the Masons to invite into membership men from a variety of denominations.

2. *Hartford Monthly*, March, 1990, p. 56.

3. Ibid.

4. "The Story of Fox's 1847-1947," *Connecticut Historical Society Bulletin*, Vol. 60, Winter/Spring 1995, 47.

Chapter Five

1. Ira Neimark, *Crossing Fifth Avenue to Bergdorf Goodman* (New York: Specialist Press International, 2006) p. 73.

2. Ibid.

3. Ibid., p. 74.

4. Address to Junior Executives, 1947.

5. Earl Elhart, *The Executive Edition of Retailing.* (December, 1938).

6. Ibid.

7. Robeert Epstein, "The Story of Fox's 1847-1947," *Connecticut Historical Society Bulletin*, Vol. 60 (Winter/ Spring 1995).

8. Neimark, p. 84.

9. Dove, "Inside a Great Store," April 12, 1955.

10. Ibid.

11. Neimark, p. 90.

12. *Saturday Review of Literature.*

13. Linda Case, "The Very Private Life of Beatrice Fox Auerbach," *Northeast Magazine of the Hartford Courant*, May 4, 1986, p. 16.

14. For several years, his program had the largest number of morning radio listeners in the United States.

15. Case, p. 15.

16. A commemorative book entitled *The Highways and Byways of Connecticut* was published by G. Fox in 1945 and contained all of the broadcast vignettes.

17. Marjorie Rafal, "Beatrice Fox Auerbach." *The Temple Bulletin of Congregation Beth Israel.* February, 2005, 12.

18. Case, p. 18.

19. Neimark, p. 87.

20. Ibid., p. 90.

21. Robert Hendrickson, *The Grand Emporium* (New York: Stein and Day, 1979), pp. 359-360.

22. Dove, "Inside a Great Store," April 12, 1955, p. 14.

23. Ibid.

24. Ibid., p. 15.

25. Case, p. 14.

26. Neimark, p. 72.

27. Ibid., p. 90.

Chapter Six

1. Epstein.

2. Stewart Onan, *The Circus Fire: A True Story of an American Tragedy* (New York: Doubleday, 2001) p. 177. *Time* magazine, September 17, 1944, ran a very powerful account of the fire entitled "Six Minutes."

Chapter Seven

1. Epstein, p. 84.

2. H. Baker cited in Duncan and Phillips, *Retailing Principles and Methods, 5th edition,* 1959.

3. Carsky, p. 222.

4. Dove, "Inside a Great Store," April 15, 1955.

5. Research has found a handful of black salespeople in New York and Boston during the 1940s.

Chapter Eight

1. *Hartford Times,* June 1945.

2. Ibid.

Chapter Nine

1. *New York Times,* November 24, 1965.

2. Pamphlet from archives of the Dodd Center, University of Connecticut.

3. Ibid.

4. Eleanor Roosevelt, address in Centinel Hill Hall, January 20, 1947.

Chapter Ten

1. Neimark, p. 99.
2. Case, p. 17.
3. Carsky, p. 226.

Chapter Eleven

1. Rafal, November, 2004.
2. Louis Sampliner, 2/27/86.

Chapter Twelve

1. James Torres Bodet. Opening Address to the International Conference on Public Education in Geneva. July, 1952.
2. William Ryan, *Hartford Times*, August 1, 1956.
3. Ibid.
4. Rafal, December 2004-January 2005.
5. Exactly why Beatrice so admired Rhodes can only be guessed. Certainly, he played a major political and economic role in colonial South Africa. While receiving a degree from Oxford, he became a

diamond miner. By 1888, Rhodes managed to solidly establish the De Beers Consolidated Mines, Ltd. In 1891, that company owned 90 percent of the world's diamond mines. He led the development of territories north of South Africa, including Zambia, Malawi, and Botswana (now Zimbabwe). He sought to unite the Boers and British in the South African parliament. He defined his policy as "equal rights for every civilized man south of the Zambezi." Although he never achieved his political visions, his business endeavors made him very prosperous. In his will, he left most of his wealth to Oxford University where the famed Rhodes Scholarship was established.

6. Case, p. 15.

7. Ibid.

8. Many of those interviewed, including Beatrice's secretary, Shirley Koplowitz, confirmed this opinion.

9. The cabin at which Mrs. Roosevelt stayed was the guest cabin, a large two-bedroom cabin, which is the only one with a view of the pool.

10. Eleanor Roosevelt, *Daily Telegraph*, July 28, 1951.

11. *Hartford Times*, June 8, 1951.

12. Beatrice went to New York City once a week, usually on a Monday. She often brought with her gifts from Auerfarm for friends and relatives, and Harry would drop them off.

13. Rena Koopman recalls her mother telling her that Beatrice traveled to Hyde Park only to find she had left the invitation at home. The security guards refused her admittance.

Chapter Thirteen

1. Carsky, p. 226.
2. In 2006, Federated acquired the May Company, and the Filene's banner, which had replaced G. Fox's, is now Macy's. In a sense, the affiliation Beatrice preferred has come to pass.
3. Case, p. 18.
4. *Hartford Courant*, December 1, 1968, 10.
5. Ibid.
6. *Hartford Times*, December 1, 1968, 8A.
7. *Hartford Courant*, December 1, 1968, 6.
8. *Hartford Times*, December 1, 1968, 8A.
9. *Hartford Courant*, December 1, 1968, 10.

Epilogue

1. Commencement program, University of Hartford, May, 1955.

2. John Trahan, head librarian at the Beatrice Fox Auerbach Library of the Wadsworth Atheneum.

3. Mary Smith, unpublished address to the Ladies Club of Courtland, New York, 1985.

4. H. Wilson Faude, "A Lost Connection," *Hartford Courant*, July 22, 2007. The article discusses in detail failures in planned urban development for Hartford.

5. Case, p. 15.

6. Publication of Congregation Beth Israel, November 2004.

7. Obituary of Dorothy Auerbach Schiro, *Hartford Courant*, December 30, 1998.

Selected Bibliography

A Century in Connecticut. Hartford, CT: G. Fox and Company, 1948.

"Angle on Her Store," *Dry Goods Economist* (December 7, 1937): 8-12.

Auerbach, Beatrice Fox, Correspondence and Journals.

Barrett, Robert. "G. Fox Customers Miss the Old Family Store." *Women's Wear Daily* (December 14, 1970): 1.

Black Women of Connecticut: Achievements Against the Odds. Hartford: The Connecticut Historical Society, 1984: 7.

Carsky, Mary and John F. Donnellan, "G. Fox: Grand Emporium." *Conference on Historical Research in Marketing and Marketing Thought.*

Case, Linda. "The Very Private Life of Beatrice Fox Auerbach," *Northeast Magazine of the Hartford Courant* (May 4, 1986): 13-23.

"Centinel Hill Hall Recalls City's Founders," *Hartford Times* (June 5, 1940).

"Corner Seat in New G. Fox Restaurant," *Hartford Courant* (July 9, 1939).

"City of Merchants," *Hartford Times* (January 1, 1942).

Dalin, David and Jonathan Rosenbaum. *Making a Life, Building a Community: A History of the Jews of Hartford.* New York: Holmes & Meier Publishers, 1997.

Dove, Roger, "Inside a Great Store," *Hartford Courant* (April 11-16, 1955).

_____. "Memories of a Hartford Retailing Matriarch," *Hartford Courant* (September 16, 1992).

Duncan D. J. and Phillips C. F. *Retailing Principles and Methods*. 5th edition. Homewood, IL: Richard D. Irwin Inc., 1959: 765-776.

"87th Anniversary Finds Fox's Near Modernity's Peak," *Hartford Courant* (December 5, 1939).

Elhart, Earl. *The Executive Edition of Retailing*. 10 (Winter/Spring, 1938).

Epstein, Robert J. "The Story of Fox's 1847-1947" *Connecticut Historical Society Bulletin*, 60 (Winter/Spring 1995).

Feinberg, Sam "The Phenomenal Mrs. Auerbach," *Hartford Courant* (July 17, 1968).

_____. "The Trio that Makes G. Fox Great," *Women's Wear Daily* (November 13, 1968) 10.

Feldman, Abraham J. *Remember the Days of Old Hartford*. (1943).

Ferry, John Williams *A History of the Department Store*. New York: Macmillan Company, 1960.

"Fox's Store Employees Get Hospital," *Hartford Courant* (February 25, 1940).

"G. Fox Basement Store to Mark 44th Year," *Hartford Courant.* (November 28, 1963): 8.

"G. Fox Expansion to Cost $6 Million," *Hartford Times* (July 13, 1956): 1.

"G. Fox & Co. Expansion to Start," *Hartford Courant* (February 8, 1956) 1, 10A.

"G. Fox of Hartford Acquired by May Co., for $40 Million," *Women's Wear Daily* (October 28, 1965): 113.

"G. Fox Moves to Complete Modernizing," *Hartford Times* (December 21, 1933).

"G. Fox Veterans Honor 19 for 25 Years Service," *Hartford Times* (May 14, 1962): 16.

Gingras, Nancy "Demise of a Special Store Will Leave a Void in Many Lives," *Hartford Courant* (November 30, 1968).

Go-Getter, internal newsletter for G. Fox employees.

Great Women in Connecticut History. Hartford, CT, The Permanent Commission on the Status of Women, 1978.

Harris, Leon. *Merchant Princes*. New York: Harper and Row, 1977.

Hendrickson, Robert. *The Grand Emporiums*. New York: Stein and Day, 1979.

"Just a Year After the Great Fire that Destroyed G. Fox & Co. Building One of the Finest Structures in New England Is Erected," *Hartford Courant* (January 27, 1918).

Lacy, John "G. Fox, a Cultural Landmark," *Hartford Courant* (January 12, 1993).

Leach, William R. "Transformations in a Culture of Consumption: Women and Department Stores, 1890-1925," *Journal of American History* 71 (2) (1984): 319-342.

"Local Store Celebrating 75th Birthday," *Hartford Courant* (March 9, 1941).

Mahoney, Thomas and Leonard Sloane. *The Great Merchants.* New York: Harper & Row, 1966.

"Modern Elevator Façade at G. Fox's," *Hartford Courant* (May 6, 1934).

"Modernity Marks Fox's Main Floor," *Hartford Courant* (September 16, 1939).

"Modernization of the Downtown Store," *Department Store Economist* (July 22-26, 1950): 106.

"Moses Fox Club Launched with 77 Charter Members," *Hartford Times* (February 5, 1940).

"Mrs. Beatrice Auerbach Dies" *Hartford Courant* (November 30, 1968).

"Mrs. Auerbach Rites Today, Civic Leader, Philanthropist." *Hartford Times* (December 1, 1968).

Neimark, Ira. *Crossing Fifth Avenue to Bergdorf Goodman* New York: Specialist Press International, 2006.

"New Cafeteria for Employees Opens at G. Fox," *Hartford Times* (June 19, 1962).

New, Irene. "The Jewish Business Woman in America," *American Jewish Historical Quarterly* 67 (1), (1976): 127-154.

Onan, Stewart. *The Circus Fire: A True Story of an American Tragedy.* New York: Doubleday, 2001.

Otto, Mary. "Fox Tearoom's Legacy: Memories of Gentility," *Hartford Courant* (January 17, 1993).

Ouelette, Jean. "The Auerbach Aura" *Hartford Monthly*, III (March, 1990).

Perry, Charles R. *The Negro in the Department Store Industry.* Philadelphia: University of Pennsylvania Press, 1971.

Rafal, Marjorie. "Beatrice Fox Auerbach" a four-part essay Hartford, CT: *The Temple Bulletin of Congregation Beth Israel* (Nov. 2004-Feb. 2005).

Reilly, Philip J. *The Old Masters of Retailing.* New York: Fairchild Publications 1966.

Rich, Richard "A New Spirit and Faith in the Future of Downtown," *Department Store Economist.* (November, 1957): 38-39, 46, 64, 111.

Sicherman, Barbara, Carol Green, H. Gene Kontron, and Harriette Walker (eds.) *Notable American Women,* Cambridge, MA: Harvard University, The Belnap Press 1977.

Silverman, Morris R. *Hartford Jews 1659-1970.* Hartford: Connecticut Historical Society, 1970.

"Six Large Stores Reduce Hours 5 to close at 5:30," *Hartford Times* (August 23, 1941).

Sloane, Leonard. "G. Fox: A Bit of Hartford History," *New York Times* (December 23, 1965): 27.

Talbott, Philip M. "Downtown Is Everybody's Business," *Department Store Economist* (November 1956): 38-39.

Tannenbaum, Ralph. "The Jewish Community in Utah," *Utah History Encyclopedia* www.media. utah.edu/UHE/jJEWISCOM.html.

"The Big Store Hustles" *Connecticut Life* (December 1963): 19-22.

Wendt, Lloyd and Herman Kogan. *Give the Lady What She Wants.* Chicago: Rand McNally, 1952.

Index

A

B